SUPER SECRETS OF THE SUCCESSFUL JOBSEEKER

Everything you need to know about finding a job in difficult times

by Simon Gray

HARRIMAN HOUSE LTD

3A Penns Road
Petersfield
Hampshire
GU32 2EW
GREAT BRITAIN

Tel: +44 (0)1730 233870
Fax: +44 (0)1730 233880
Email: enquiries@harriman-house.com
Website: www.harriman-house.com

First published in Great Britain in 2012

ISBN: 9780857192486

British Library Cataloguing in Publication Data
A CIP catalogue record for this book can be obtained from the British Library.

Set in Minion Pro and Gotham Narrow.

Printed and bound in the UK by CPI Antony Rowe.

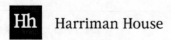

Contents

eBook edition

As a buyer of the print edition of *Super Secrets of the Successful Jobseeker* you can now download the eBook edition free of charge to read on an eBook reader, your smartphone or your computer. Simply go to:

http://ebooks.harriman-house.com/successfuljobseeker

or point your smartphone at the QRC below.

You can then register and download your eBook copy of the book.

www.harriman-house.com

About the Author

Simon Gray began his recruitment career in 1999. Ten years later, he jointly founded Cherry Professional Limited, a recruitment business dedicated to providing the best career advice to jobseekers. Simon is also a Chartered Accountant having qualified with KPMG which adds to his skills as a professional recruiter. These two areas of expertise both call for rigour and a sense of detail which he also applies away from the office as an accomplished Martial Artist.

Simon is an experienced commentator, regularly quoted on BBC Radio and in other media, offering tips to both jobseekers and employers.

In 'Super Secrets of the Successful Jobseeker', he combines his mental discipline, understanding of the psychology of people and expert knowledge of the job market to give the jobseeker that all important edge.

Summary

With high unemployment and jobseekers fighting for fewer and fewer jobs it's never been more important to get an edge when looking for that next career move. The right experience and qualifications, a good CV and a nicely worded covering letter are no longer enough – they are the bare minimum!

In this book, Simon Gray, a qualified Chartered Accountant and experienced recruiter, explains how to get ahead, what to do and what not to do to win in the highly competitive job race. He also explores the psychology of looking for a job and divulges his revolutionary techniques to get noticed and employed in a crowded market.

Whether you're out of work or planning to change career, this is the book you can't afford not to read!

Introduction

"Life is all about effective relationships – what could be simpler or more complicated than that."

Simon Gray

There is lots of advice out there on how to find a job – some good and some bad. The majority of texts focus on how to write a great CV, as if this was the most important and only thing to do. Of course it is important, but it only scratches the surface. It's the tip of the iceberg on what can be the long hard road to finding a job.

I've interviewed hundreds, if not thousands, of candidates and almost all of them focus too much on their CV, worrying about its length, layout and content. Clearly a good CV is massively important, but it won't find you your next job. It won't identify a job opportunity, go on an interview or get your personality across. No, I'm sorry it won't!

I've sat across the table from highly experienced individuals in their field, far cleverer than I, but when faced with the challenge of finding a new job they appear lost, confused and even angry.

The feedback from courses I have run highlighting the content of this book has been really positive. I have delivered it to college students and experienced professionals, both of whom face the same challenges, but at different stages of their career. It is for these individuals, and everyone else who is finding it hard to secure that next move, that I've written this book. My aim is to get this information out to those who need it most in an easily accessible, clear and concise format. This is not a weighty text – it doesn't need to be. Less is often more and as with writing a great CV, if it doesn't add value it should be left out and it has been here.

It doesn't matter what type of job you are looking for or in what sector – this book has advice for all. This is not a boring textbook or a list of what to do or not do. Let's face it, we've all read those books, but how many have you actually finished? I still have a pile next to my bed and I'm running out of bookmarks.

This isn't theory – it's real and practical advice that you can start implementing within your job search game. Because like it or not, that's what it is... one big, fat, unadulterated game – and those that play it best are those who win.

Why do footballers, politicians or business people look and often act the same? Is it because we have an expectation that they should be that way? Do all footballers like expensive cars? Probably not... but if David Beckham turned up to training in a Ford Fiesta, what would his fellow players or manager think or, worst still, say?

We all have a desire to fit in, but there is fitting in and *fitting in*.

In Japan they have a saying that if a nail stands out it should be hammered down, meaning those that stand out are quickly put back into line. It should be noted that they also have a word, 'Karoshi', meaning death from overwork (this is considered honourable) – so we won't pay too much attention!

The secret is to fit in but also to stand out at the same time – to be recognised and remembered for the right reasons. We live in a society of monotony and what makes us stand up and pay attention is something slightly different or unique in some way... something out of the ordinary.

How often do you arrive home from work and when asked to recall the events of the day highlight everything that normally happens or was expected? Do I say to my wife, I drove to work today and arrived on time, or would I mention the journey to work only if I'd been late due to an accident or traffic jam or both? It's still the journey to work, the normal route in the same car but something stood out, made me pay attention and as such, firmly lodged a place in my memory.

How often have you driven to work and not even remembered the journey? Worrying isn't it – all those drivers out there not even thinking about what they are doing or where they are going! We all walk around in a fog of routine, the details of which we don't remember because it's just not that exciting. What stands out a bit gets remembered, but what stands out too much is just odd; there's a fine line and getting the balance just right takes practice.

The techniques I outline throughout this book are to help you fit in and also stand out. They tread that fine line between understated and overpowering. They help you to be you and someone that is remembered ahead of the competition.

Your life and your job search is about you, so:

Yell

Out

Uniqueness!

If we were share dealing this would be insider trading. This is the inside track, the tricks of the trade to put you the jobseeker at the top of your game. This is *Super Secrets of the Successful Jobseeker*.

Congratulations – you are already one step closer to finding your next job – so let's begin!

Attack from the HIGH GROUND

We've all seen the movies where the army general arrives at the battleground early to pick the best spot from which to launch the attack. Setting up camp at the top of a hill with the sun behind you makes it harder for your adversary to reach you and easier for you to launch the full force of your attack on your enemy. Attacking from the high ground is important to the jobseeker too – the high ground here is your mental state.

I've interviewed many people looking for a job over the years and they tend to fall into two categories. Let's take a look at Bill and Bob, two purely fictional – but typical – characters:

Bill is positive, motivated and driven, but just needs guidance in a few areas. He asks lots of questions about what to do, how to do it and is very engaging and enthusiastic. He knows he doesn't have all the answers and his mind is open to fresh and new ideas of how to find his next job.

Bob is negative, depressed and down on his luck. He's tried everything (or so he thinks) to find a job without success. He has no questions, feels hard done by and has a huge chip on his shoulder, which is clearly visible to all but him.

So what separates Bill and Bob from one another? Not in terms of how they come across, but slightly more cryptic than that. Well the answer is quite simple – it's TIME. You see, Bill and Bob are the same person separated by time.

Bill has just come on to the job market whereas Bob has been looking for some time now – why Bob has not been successful is not the point here, the point is that he has been looking for a while.

So, who is an employer most likely to hire? Who would you prefer to go for a beer with? The answer is Bill, of course – unless you like to hang out with negative and downbeat people. Bob is battle weary, fatigued and is cramping his own style. Each rejection further fuels his fire of negativity and he believes that his cause is lost.

His expectation is that he will be rejected time and time again and he is right; because he believes this to be the case, it is a prime example of self-fulfilling expectations! Remember, our beliefs shape our actions, which in turn deliver us our reality. So how does Bob get back to Bill, or better still how does Bill prevent himself from becoming Bob in the first place – simply put, how does Bill stay Bill?

Well here goes:

- Realise that rejection is part of the process.
- Understand that you only need one job, not every job you go for.
- Don't make finding your next job your sole focus.
- Write a strategic business plan with targets and action points to find your next job (see Chapter 4).
- Realise that the interview process is a two-way street and change your thinking accordingly (see Chapter 8).

So now let's touch on these areas in more detail.

You can't win them all – rejection is just part of the process on the journey to finding your next role. Accept this from the outset and welcome it when it comes. Rejection doesn't mean you're a bad candidate, it doesn't mean your skills weren't up to scratch, it just means that for whatever reason on that occasion it wasn't meant to be! Indeed, rejection is essential as it gives you experience. When it comes, delve deeper and ask for feedback – what is it that you can take away positively from the experience that can help you next time?

Remember that you only need one job. Rejection along the way is experience gained that helps you get the job that's meant for you – it's character building. Very few people are offered a job by the first company they approach or interview with – unfortunately, that's just not the way it works. The successful jobseeker realises this and accepts it from the outset – it's all part of the game. As Rudyard Kipling advises in his famous poem: "If you can keep your head while all around you are losing theirs…" Accept rejection as part of the experience and keep your head for next time.

Many jobseekers fall into the trap of making finding their next job their sole and total focus – this is a big mistake. We all need balance in our lives and this holds true for the jobseeker too. Bill turns into Bob because he sits at home searching the internet for his next job. He does this morning, noon and night in the hope that more effort (I wouldn't class this as effort, well certainly not the right effort – but more on that later) means a bigger chance of reward… but this is not so. With his sole focus on finding his next job it's no wonder he gets frustrated and down. Without setting his plan he has inadvertently planned to fail, which brings me on to the next point.

The successful jobseeker knows that planning is everything. If you don't have a set plan you don't know what you should be doing and when. More importantly, you don't know when to step away from your quest before it consumes you and those around you. We'll discuss this in detail in Chapter 4, but note here that a well thought out plan that is rigidly followed is massively important to your mental well-being, confidence and subsequently your ability to find your next position.

Finally, remember it's a two-way street. Too many jobseekers focus solely on what an employer thinks about them without ever stepping back and asking themselves what they think of the employer. It's no wonder they take feedback to heart; they have put themselves at the mercy of the mighty employer without any consideration for their own feelings and thoughts. Remember, it's a two-way qualification process and this shift in your mental thought process can have profound effects on your success in the job market.

To illustrate this point think about two people, introduced through a mutual friend, who go on a date – let's call them John and Jacky.

John is desperate to find love and through-out the date his only concern is what Jacky thinks of him – he tries too hard and Jacky finds this uncomfortable. Jacky on the other hand goes along with no expectations; she's keen to find out about John and see if he is the type of guy she could get on with. After the date John wants to see Jacky again but Jacky is not so sure.

This situation sounds familiar because it goes on in all aspects of life. Trying too hard and concentrating solely on the end result is a surefire route to failure. Instead, focus on the process, not the outcome. With a planned and disciplined process the outcome is guaranteed – you may not know when, but as sure as night follows day, a well executed plan will deliver the outcome you desire.

Responsibility is also a key concept that needs to be addressed. As human beings we are masters of making excuses:

"It's not my fault!"

"It's just how things are!"

"I can't help it!"

"There's nothing I can do!"

"Such and such hasn't done anything to help me!"

"Such and such has really let me down!"

Sound familiar? Well guess what – it's total drivel; complete and utter nonsense and it is counterproductive to getting on in life.

You and you alone have total responsibility for everything that happens in your life and this includes finding your next job. Clearly we can't control everything that happens to us – we can't stop the rain or magically make the sun come out – but we can control how we feel about and react to things. We have sole responsibility for our minds, attitudes and what we do or don't do. We have choices and we can choose how we feel and choose what actions we will take. The problem is that excuses conveniently get in the way, and that's because excuses are a great way to avoid responsibility. Finding your next job is totally and utterly your responsibility. This is so important I'll say it again: **Finding your next job is totally and utterly your responsibility!**

How you feel is your choice. How you act is your choice. Understand this now and you are one step closer to successfully finding your next job!

Understanding a TOUGH MARKET

We all know the saying that knowledge is power – well the good news is that it actually is! The more you know about your environment the better you can adapt to it. Just as the primitive man built shelter for warmth and made spears for hunting, the successful jobseeker must build a set of effective tools for finding that next role.

The jobseeker who knows and understands the market is better able to adapt to that market. I have interviewed a number of people recently who have been in secure jobs for many years but have just come back onto the job market through redundancy. Their expectations are unrealistic; they are stuck in a time warp of when they last looked for a job, when they probably found it fairly easy.

It's a bit like a prisoner newly released from prison after serving a 20-year stretch – their surroundings are unfamiliar, they've never heard of or seen an iPhone or iPad and they feel lost and confused!

There are two approaches to this:

1. The deluded, or 'ostrich method', where they bury their head in the sand and convince themselves that life is as it was back then.

2. The informed approach, where they realise times have changed and go out of their way to better understand the job market, so that they are best placed to attack it in the right way.

With so many people unemployed in the UK, across Europe and throughout the rest of the world, the law of demand and supply tells us that finding a job is going to be difficult. With a lower demand (the number of vacancies or put another way, employers actively hiring) and increased supply (the number of jobseekers on the market) there has been downward pressure on price (salaries in this case) and jobseekers now have to work harder and be smarter to get a foot in the door.

So let's take a closer look at what employers and jobseekers are currently thinking.

Employers

- There are lots of great candidates out there with the skills we need.

- We don't need to try too hard to find them because there are lots of them.

- We don't need to rush ourselves, as we are unlikely to be in competition for their skills.

- They (the candidates) need us more than we need them.

- We won't hire unless it's absolutely essential – we don't want to take an unnecessary risk or incur unnecessary cost.

- Candidates should be grateful for a job.

In summary they are thinking – WE HAVE THE POWER!

Jobseekers

- There aren't many jobs out there; it's going to be really tough to find a job.

- I'm going to have to work really hard to find a job and I'm not guaranteed to find one – is there any point?

- I need a job more than any employer is going to need me.

- I should be grateful for any job I'm offered.

- I'll take anything I'm offered on whatever salary – I'm desperate.

In summary they are thinking – WE HAVE NO POWER!

You can only control what you can control; you can't hope to change the mindset of employers in general – clearly that's just not going to happen. You can however, with a deeper understanding of what they are thinking, make your skills and experience indispensable using reverse psychology to tip the balance of power in your favour (more on this in Chapters 7 and 8).

Remember who your competition is – yes, that's right it's other jobseekers. If you start to think and act differently, aren't you already at a distinct advantage? You've just jumped right to the front of the queue and are equipped for battle!

I appreciate that at the time you read this book the job market may look very different again, but this is not the point. The point is that whatever the market looks like and however people are thinking, you need to understand it so that you can better prepare yourself for the journey ahead and the challenge of finding your next job.

Research

You may think this sounds all well and good, but are still wondering how you can find out what the market looks like and even, what is the market? On a large scale the market is the national employment situation, or international situation if you are geographically mobile. But delve deeper – aren't you restricted by sector and location? For example, let's get back to Bob (you met him in Chapter 1) who is an accountant and lives in Nottingham – what's his market?

Bob's market is accounting and finance jobs in Nottingham, Derby and Leicester, as he is prepared to travel anywhere in the East Midlands. Great – but what does Bob need to do next to better understand the market so that he can better attack it?

1. Read the local press to find out what's happening in the local economy – the thickness of the jobs paper can be a good indicator as to the level of hiring activity in the market.

2. Internet – search job boards for opportunities in his locality and in his sector. What's happening and what skills are employers looking for?

3. Talk to the professionals – set up meetings with local recruitment businesses that specialise in his sector. Ask their advice on what's happening, skills sought after and salary levels.

4. Map the businesses across the region; who are the larger businesses and who are the up and coming SMEs (small and medium-sized enterprises)?

Bob then needs to document what he's learnt, as this will form part of his business plan to attack the market – more on that later. The point is that Bob and you the jobseeker need to have realistic expectations; you need to understand the market and environment you are living in.

Let's think of it another way... Bob is planning a weekend away with his family. He's off walking in the countryside and has really been looking forward to the break. If you were in Bob's shoes, is there anything you would do before packing and leaving? Well... you could check the weather forecast. If it looks like rain it's probably a good idea to pack a raincoat and boots! If it does then rain, a much more enjoyable weekend will be had, having packed the right equipment!

With a clear picture of how things are, you are far better informed and more empowered to plan your attack and find your next position.

Constructing a SUPER CV

When people talk about finding a job, the first thought process or topic of conversation is generally about getting their CV updated.

STOP right there!

Updating a CV in the world of the jobseeker is a criminal offence punishable by a long and painful period of unemployment. Compare it to decorating the house and painting over the cracks or existing wallpaper – it might look good on the surface but sooner or later the cracks will start to show through and the wallpaper will start to peel.

DON'T UPDATE – START FROM SCRATCH!

A well written and constructed CV starts with a blank piece of paper or in the modern world we live in, a blank Word document. Don't be lazy; understand the importance of a CV, as it's the most important document you will write this year – that is if you are serious about finding a job.

The super successful jobseeker knows a CV is important because:

1. It's the first introduction of you to an employer – the first opportunity an employer has to make a judgement on you and your skills.

2. There are lots and lots of CVs out there in the market, so time and effort to make yours stand out is time well spent.

Beware of false prophets

I've heard many a horror story of candidates spending up to £500 (and sometimes even more) for someone they have never met and who knows very little about them to write their CV!

STOP – alarm bells should be ringing now – let's look at that again – someone they've NEVER MET and who knows VERY LITTLE about them!

A CV is a highly personal document – it's about YOU the writer, no one else. No one is more qualified to write this document than you – FACT! As such, beware of false prophets and people promising to write a CV like no other CV you've ever seen – if it sounds too good to be true (and costs you money in the process) it probably is!

Why invest the time to write a great CV?

Why do employers ask for a CV and why are jobseekers required to spend time and effort preparing one?

It's the best way yet that employers have come up with to filter initial candidate enquiries and to make a decision on who to invite for an interview. Is it the best method to find the right person? Well, in truth it's probably not. Just because someone is skilled at writing a CV it doesn't necessarily make them the best at their job nor does it get across their personality, which alongside skills is the key criteria employers make their hiring decisions on.

In the recruitment industry we spend lots of time meeting with jobseekers, many of whom have poor CVs but are actually really good at what they do and come across fantastically in person – they are highly employable. Recruitment is our industry, so we are prepared to invest the time to remedy their CV; a strong CV backed up by a well prepared and highly personable candidate is how we make our money.

However, an employer hasn't the time to meet lots of people, so at the outset relies solely on the quality of a candidate's CV. Until someone comes up with a better idea to gauge suitability for a position at the outset, we are stuck with the CV – so we better make it a good one.

So, before going any further let's address the fundamental question – what is the purpose of a CV?

Is it to document your life history?

Is it to demonstrate your command of the English language and vocabulary knowledge?

NO!

A CV has only one purpose and that is to win you an interview.

I use the word 'win' here deliberately. Remember, in most industries a CV won't get you a job – your performance at interview will (more on this in Chapter 9). In a highly competitive job market, it is what it says it is – a competition! To win the competition, your CV needs to stand out; it needs to be memorable and it needs to have impact. But wait – need is not a strong enough word here.

In a highly competitive job market your CV:

- MUST stand out.
- MUST be memorable.
- MUST have impact.

These are the three Ms of an effective CV.

Let me ask you a question. When you are looking for that all important book to read in preparation for your holiday, what do you do? In visiting a bookstore (or similarly browsing titles on the internet) do you flick through the pages and read the summary on the back? When you are deciding on the next movie to watch at the cinema do you read the reviews or better still watch the trailers?

If you answered YES to both you are already part way there to writing a great CV.

The book publishers and film studios look to captivate your interest in a very short period of time so that you will buy the book or pay to watch the film. They have only a short period of time because, let's face it, we're all busy and there are so many other titles to choose from.

It's exactly the same with your CV. The definition of CV – Curriculum Vitae, namely 'Course of Life' or 'Life's Journey' – is fundamentally flawed. The last thing an employer wants to read is your autobiography in every minute detail – they're simply not that interested, nor do they have the time. Remember, your CV is a sales document, a memorandum of your career to date. It is most definitely not an exhaustive list of everything you have done!

Who reads a CV?

In truth, there is no one particular way to write a CV and no hard and fast rules on structure – a lot depends on the answer to the following questions:

- Who is your target audience, i.e. who is going to read it?

- What are they looking for?

- Think about the last time you wrote your CV. Did you stop and think about these two key questions before putting pen to paper or finger to keyboard? If not, why not?

- When a teacher instructs a class, do they tailor the lesson to the level of their students or just cover what they want to? A good teacher wants their students to get the most out of a class and this is what you need to do with your CV. You need to speak the language of your audience and speak it well!

- If you don't know who you are writing your CV for, how can you send the right message in the right style? The answer is you can't – you must address the reader.

Let's bring back Bill, the jobseeker who is trying not to turn into Bob (that's right – he's sticking to the high ground). Bill is sending his CV to an employer who has advertised a position in a newspaper. Does it make a difference whether he is required to send his CV to the Human Resources Director or to the Managing Partner of the firm? Absolutely it does – remember you must address the reader.

Bill (like Bob) is a qualified accountant and has worked in the industry for a number of years. He is technically up to speed and could be tempted to put technical jargon in his CV to try and impress! Although the Managing Partner (a qualified accountant too) would understand such jargon, the Human Resources Director may not, as a result of not possessing a professional accounting qualification.

This is one of the reasons why I recommend not using jargon or technical terms in a CV. I recommend that jobseekers give their CV to someone who doesn't understand their profession and ask them to read it and then summarise what they do. If the reader doesn't get it or doesn't understand the content then all that time and effort in preparation is wasted.

Let's face it, we're all a bit lazy from time to time and if we don't understand something it's sometimes easier to put it to one side and look at something else. An employer with plenty of other options in the form of other CVs may simply bypass yours if it is too difficult to comprehend, even though you may be the best candidate for the job.

To make life even more difficult, guess how long an employer spends actually reading your CV? Do you think they read it from start to finish and then once more just to check they've not missed anything? Unfortunately not – not in this market anyway! In my experience an employer makes a judgment on your CV in about 15 seconds (they certainly don't read it from start to finish). That's all the time you get to make a great first impression!

The CV read has two waves – Wave 1 and Wave 2 – and our aim is to make it to Wave 2. Let's discuss each in turn:

Wave 1

The employer has a pile of CVs to wade through. Recruiting is not their fulltime job so they want to get through the pile as quickly as possible and get back to doing what they really want to be doing – running their business and making money!

(Having the right people in a business doing the right things is possibly one of the most important things for the success of any business but it is often the thing that gets rushed and done once a spare few minutes is found).

In Wave 1 the employer skim reads the CVs and forms three piles:

1. YES – looks interesting, will read a bit more later and perhaps invite in for interview.

2. NO – next stop the shredder or bin, whichever is close at hand.

3. MAYBE – the secondary NO pile, which also ends up in the shredder or bin.

Wave 2

In Wave 2 the employer reads through the YES pile and creates a shortlist to invite for interview.

Clearly if you don't make the YES pile you don't get the interview, so all of our attention needs to be towards getting in the YES pile.

The NO pile speaks for itself and the MAYBE pile with the time pressures of the busy world we live in also ends up as another NO pile as employers rarely get round to having a proper look through it.

So enough of the background – how do you write the best CV you can possibly write?

Well, as discussed earlier, start with a blank piece of paper or Word document, a pen or keyboard and a quiet room where you won't be disturbed.

Now write these words at the top of the page:

Something different/add value!

Aside from factual information, such as your name, address and contact details, everything on your CV should fight for the right to be there. Imagine that each line of text costs you money and ask yourself, would you pay to include that line in your CV? If it isn't something different or doesn't add value then leave it out.

Employers who put you in the YES pile are looking for something different, something interesting that makes them stand up and take notice – something that gets their attention. They are also looking for evidence of you adding value in previous companies – but why?

Well, because it's the best evidence they've got or are going to get on your ability to do the same for them.

What should a CV contain?

Taking into account all I've said so far, a CV needs to contain the necessary information for an employer to make an informed decision quickly and efficiently.

A detailed CV template can be found in the Appendix, but here I'll discuss the main content, which can be summarised as follows:

- Name
- Current residence and where you are relocating to and/or geographical flexibility if relevant
- School/university education (include grades) and place of study
- Professional qualifications, including exam record if relevant
- Languages and level of ability
- Work experience for each role you have held, including for each:
    - Company/organisation and description
    - Job title
    - Responsibilities and achievements

- Computer/IT skills including level of ability with each system
- Hobbies and interests and to what level.

Let's delve a little deeper into each of these areas.

Name

This is the easy bit! Your full name and if it's not clear which is your surname/family name then underline it.

Residence

Where do you live and how geographically flexible are you?

If Bill is applying for a job in London but he currently works in Nottingham, then London employers who would prefer to hire someone local may not consider his application. What the London employers don't know is that Bill is relocating to London and has already committed to doing this as he's bought a house – they don't know this because it's not on his CV.

Bill is advised to put:

Currently Nottingham – moving to London on… (include the date) – house already purchased.

School/university education

Include school education, together with subjects if they are relevant to the job you are applying for and grades. If you have a degree make sure you say where you studied and also the class of degree obtained.

Professional qualifications

Include the full title of the qualification you hold and if you passed all exams first time, include this too. Make sure that if holding your qualification requires you to pay annual subscriptions that you are up to date, as this will avoid any qualification checking issues further down the line.

Work experience

Company/organisation and description

Employers will be interested to see who you have worked for and for how long. Even if a business you have worked for is well known, it may not be well known to the employer you are applying to – don't assume anything!

Size and sector of business has become increasingly important in recent times. What this means is that if you've worked in the technology sector (in whatever profession) that your experience will be very attractive to other businesses in the technology sector, as it's likely you'd arrive on day one with some knowledge. Similarly, if you have experience working in large corporate businesses your experience will be attractive to other large corporates.

Employers are looking to mitigate risk and cost as much as possible. If they can hire someone who has worked in their sector for a similar sized business, then why wouldn't they? If they take a gamble on someone from outside the sector then there could be a risk that they may not stick it, or that it might not work out for a whole host of other reasons. If things don't work out it means financial cost, as well as cost in terms of time lost, as the employer is effectively back to square one.

Job title

When an employer scans your CV, as well as noting where you've worked they will also focus on what your role was there. A job title can say a lot about your experience to date and much is assumed by an employer when reading your job title.

The CV template in the Appendix shows two roles for the same company. The purpose of this is to show promotion, particularly if you have worked for the same business for a number of years.

Promotion shows you were valuable, good at your job and as such were deserving of additional responsibility and the associated salary increase!

Responsibilities and achievements

Jobseekers often think of responsibilities and achievements as one and the same but they are very, very different. By getting them confused the importance of each is diluted and the impact they can have on your CV is reduced.

Remember *something different/add value* – it's written at the top of your page. Well, this is where you have the first real opportunity on your CV to show why you are different, where you have added value and why you should be invited for interview.

So let's get back to the distinction between responsibilities and achievements – any ideas?

Let's break it down and use an example to illustrate the point.

If I said to you – *"I'm a dustbin man, what are my responsibilities?"* What would you say? I'm guessing you'd have a reasonable idea, one of which might be:

"Collecting rubbish from residential homes and businesses across Nottinghamshire."

But what about my achievements? Do you have any ideas about those? No you won't, as I haven't told you yet. You see achievements are specific to my ability in my job and go above and beyond what you would expect me to be doing or to have done.

For example, one of my achievements could be:

Hold a 100% safety record over a ten year period.

Do you see how this differs? The achievement goes above and beyond – it takes a responsibility and gives it added value. It distinguishes you from your competition, namely other jobseekers who will be doing similar jobs and have similar skills and experience.

Whatever your vocation and whatever your industry, achievements are absolutely key!

Let's extend achievements a bit further and link them to interview technique, which we will come on to in Chapter 8 where we'll cover competency based interviews – just note for the moment that what we're about to do now in constructing achievements will serve you well at interview.

Are you READY now to create some powerful achievements that will light up your CV and set you apart from the competition?

That's are you READY? Or better written as:

REA – *REA*lity: Think about something you are particularly proud of doing at work and think about the situation or **REA**lity at the outset.

DY – *D*id *Y*ou do? Next, think – what **D**id **Y**ou do, that's YOU not WE, what **D**id **Y**ou do?

? – Finally think – well, so what? What was the result and, better still, can you quantify it to give it impact? Numbers have power and stand out on a CV, so if you can use them then do so.

For example, an achievement from my own CV:

I was promoted to recruit qualified accountants across the Derbyshire region (**REA**). I mapped out the client base across the region and made contact with each business in turn to establish who was the principal recruiter (**DY**). Within the first 12 months of taking on this new role I had established numerous new relationships which generated an additional £200k revenue for the company(**?**)

The achievement has impact! It shows my start position, what I did to add value and the result – it gets my point across clearly and concisely.

Picking the right achievements also tells the employer what you want to talk about at interview and prompts them to ask the right questions!

Computer/IT skills

Whatever your profession, these days you are more than likely required to use a computer or something that is supposed to (but sometimes doesn't) make life easier.

Employers are keen to see how good you are with computers and IT systems for a couple of reasons:

- They don't want to spend too much time training you – if you have reasonable IT skills then you'll more than likely pick their system up quickly.

- If you've used their operating system before, particularly to a reasonable level, you might be able to add value and/or make improvements to their existing system set up.

Detail the system you have used, your level of expertise with that system and also the length of time you used it for.

Let's say for example that I have used Sage (a well known accounting system). If I just put Sage on my CV it doesn't really say too much, does it?

How about, if I put:

Sage Line 50 – Advanced level – 5 years experience – completed a two day Super User course.

Says a lot more doesn't it?

Thinking back to achievements – if you have implemented, developed or improved a system then don't keep it a secret, use it as one of your achievements.

Hobbies and interests

This is often a hotly debated area of a CV – to include or not to include?

Let me ask you a quick question – do you prefer to be at work or at home? Or put more obviously – do you prefer work or leisure? Now, I appreciate that some people prefer work to leisure time, but most people prefer their own free time for one simple reason – they can do what they want when they want (within reason of course)! At work there are restrictions – a start and finish time being two of many more.

So let me get to the point – if leisure or free time is preferred by most people to time spent at work but they do nothing with it, what does that tell you about a person? Put another way – if someone can't get motivated to do something with their free time, how likely are they to get motivated about the time they spend at work?

One of my pet hates is seeing 'reading' as a hobby or interest on a CV. This tells me nothing and adds no value. Be specific and tell the reader of your CV what you are currently reading – this is far more interesting and providing it's quality reading material is much more impressive!

Hobbies and interests on a CV is a chance to show you are interested in something and have a passion in life. Furthermore, it's a chance to get in a few more achievements – remember achievements and how important they are? Are you **READY?**

If your hobby is running, have you completed any half or full marathons? Which ones and what was your best time? Think about it and expand your hobbies and interests to make them achievements in their own right!

Can you guess what an employer's favourite game is?

Monopoly…?

Yes, maybe – particularly if they are in the housing/construction sector.

Cluedo…?

Mmm, possibly if they are in the police or a law firm.

But actually it's SNAP! Yes, SNAP! For those of you not familiar with SNAP – it's a card game that involves matching cards. But how do they play SNAP and what are they matching your CV to? Well, most employers before they begin recruiting for any position, mentally – or more commonly in a document known as a job specification or role profile – list what the successful candidate needs to be able to do and what kind of person they are looking for.

A typical job specification has three elements:

1. A list of skills needed to perform the job successfully.

2. Any necessary qualifications.

3. Some narrative describing the type of person sought, with emphasis on personality traits.

What this means is that your CV, to give you the best possible chance of being put on the YES pile and invited in for interview, should match the job description as closely as possible. Help the employer play their game of SNAP and highlight the skills, experience and qualifications they are looking for. The easiest and best way to do this is to request a copy of the job description in advance of sending your CV. It's as easy as reviewing the role profile on the internet or picking up the phone to the employer or recruiter and asking them to send you a copy! You can then tailor and tweak your generic or master CV to highlight the specific areas relevant and most important to the role. This additional stage of preparation can pay huge dividends and win you that interview – so make sure you do it!

There are things on your CV that you absolutely must get right; there's no excuse for getting them wrong. Although simple and downright obvious, they are mentioned here as I see so many CVs where people have plain and simply messed them up!

Spelling and grammar – There is no excuse for misspelling or poor grammar. Get this wrong and it tells an employer you are sloppy and don't care. Spell check, proof read and then spell check again!

Third person – Write your CV in the third person and not the first. For example, 'Responsible for…' and not 'I was responsible for…' – the latter can be very annoying!

White space – Use lots of white space. Blocky text clumped together is hard and sometimes painful to read. Make sure you split things up and use headings and bullet points.

CV FAQs

Finally, in this chapter I'll highlight the most frequently asked questions regarding CVs.

I get asked these all the time and as I've not covered them so far, chances are they're on the tip of your tongue.

Here goes:

Should I include a covering letter with my CV?

This depends on what's asked for. If an employer requests a covering letter then you must include one – anything less is a simple failure to follow instructions!

Remember though, your CV should stand on its own two feet as a complete document that tells the reader that they absolutely have to interview you. Any covering letter should be very brief and not a duplication of your CV – there's simply no point, it's just extra stuff for the employer to wade through – trust me, they're probably doing enough wading already!

It should highlight to the addressee the most important and relevant achievement on your CV and clearly express your interest in their company and the role on offer.

Do I include a personal summary at the top of my CV?

As a professional recruiter I hate personal summaries for two reasons. Firstly, they are not factual – 'a conscientious and capable individual with excellent analytical ability and strong interpersonal skills' – it tells me nothing concrete and is just nonsense! Secondly, it pushes the real value in your CV, your responsibilities and achievements, further down the page. Don't make the reader wade through mud before they reach golden sand or they might turn round and head home!

Should I attach a photo?

Unless you are a fashion model, what you look like says nothing about your ability to do a job. Enough said on this subject!

How long should my CV be?

In my opinion there is no hard and fast rule. Your CV should be as long as it needs to be. Remember, every word and every sentence should fight for the right to be there – if it doesn't add value then take it out.

As a rule of thumb an employer or recruiter will rarely get past page three so I'd question the rationale behind anything longer. Remember that less is more; it takes less time to read but is far more powerful!

Setting your ROAD MAP

I t's the weekend, the sun is shining and you've packed up the car and are ready for the off. You turn the key in the ignition, the engine jumps to life and you begin your journey. But wait... where are you going? Have you thought about it, have you planned the route? Do you know the end destination and what to expect when you get there? What will the weather be like, have you packed the right clothes and where will you sleep tonight?

The reality is that most things in life require some planning. Don't get me wrong, some people – normally the adventurous type – leave the house without a clear plan for the day and may have a thoroughly enjoyable time. However, as a serious jobseeker you can't afford to leave things to chance and you definitely need a plan. Setting out on your job quest without a plan is planning to fail and you have no intention of failing!

Let's take a step back and think about what you might have done before setting out on your weekend away.

You probably:

- Did some research on the internet, to decide where you'd like to go.

- Pulled out a map, printed off directions or noted down an address to enter into the sat nav.

- Identified places along the way to stop and take a rest, particularly if it's likely to be a long journey.

Most people would do all of these things without thinking when setting off on a journey, so why is it that the quest to find a job is often a haphazard and random series of actions without clear direction that leaves things to chance. Think about it – if you don't know where you are going, how are you ever going to get there?

Whether you are in a job and looking for your next career move or out of work and keen to find employment, finding your next position can be a full-time job in itself. Clearly, if you are in work you have less time to devote to finding your next move but the principles of 'setting your road map' are exactly the same as if you're out of work.

Before I get into the detail, a couple of important home truths:

1. You already have a job whether you are in employment or not! You are the Managing Director of your own business. Yes, like it or not, you're the boss of your very own company called FINDING A JOB LTD.

2. Your company has no employees apart from you. That's right, the buck stops with you and as sole owner, director and manager you have responsibility for everything that happens and also everything that doesn't happen.

These two points are so obvious, yet so easily forgotten. How easy it is to blame everything and everyone for anything and everything when in actual fact it all boils down to you!

So let's get down to business and yes, I mean business. Remember you're the Managing Director of FINDING A JOB LTD. As the boss of this business you need a plan and a good one at that. Ever heard of a business obtaining a loan from a bank without a business plan? Or put another way, would you lend money to a complete stranger without knowing what it was for and having a pretty good guarantee that you'd get it back? Just as you research your destination, obtain directions and identify stop off points ahead of any journey, you set your business plan for FINDING A JOB LTD at the outset.

So now, let's take a look at this plan, build it on solid foundations, identify its components and then carry it through:

- Build your plan on solid foundations
- Identify the components
- Carry it through.

Now let's take a closer look at each of these areas.

Solid foundations

Solid foundations are the building blocks of any house and they are also the building blocks of your business plan. These are higher level things that need to be decided and set at the outset and on which all the detail of your plan rests.

Let's look at what comprises these solid foundations in more detail.

Identify the destination

What's your destination and the ultimate goal of your business plan?

As you're reading this book, I'll hazard a guess and say it's to find a job. If it's not then you're reading the wrong book and you have my permission to put this one down and choose another.

So, we're agreed that your destination and ultimate goal is to find a new job but why, with whom and what type? It may sound silly but drilling down and answering these three questions helps focus you on your quest and brings your destination to life.

Getting back to that journey for a moment…imagine your destination is New York. You're not going to New York for New York's sake, you're going for a holiday, you want to see Central Park, the Statue of Liberty and the Empire State Building. In addition, you plan to take a trip on the Staten Island Ferry and shop at Macy's. You're interested in the detail and because you're interested in the detail your destination comes to life – you're excited, motivated and ready for it!

Why are you looking for a job?

You may have been made redundant and be down on your luck, but that's not why you're looking for a job. No future employer wants to hear a sob story, what's done is done and they're not interested in that. You're looking for a job because you have skills to offer and can add value to a future employer's business.

If you're looking to move jobs, you must identify similar reasons that focus on the positive and the future.

Who do you want to work for?

There are thousands and thousands of companies out there; too many to mention and too many for you to focus on all at once, so you need to get focused and decide what type and size of business you want to work for and in what locality.

If you have experience in a particular sector this is a great starting point and if you've worked previously for smaller businesses, it makes sense to target these first.

There is a balance to be struck between where you might like to work and where your skills fit best. I might want to give up my career in recruitment and play football for Manchester United, but as I'm terrible at football it's fairly unlikely.

What type of job do you want?

Similarly, there is a balance between the type of job you want and the skills you have to offer. There may be additional responsibilities or challenges you are looking for in your next role that develop the skills and experience you have to date, which you need to think about now.

I often interview candidates who tell me they've had enough of what they're doing and want to do something completely different. I ask them why someone would want to employ them to do something they've never done before – surely that's a big risk and unlikely in a highly competitive job market?

Normally the employer gets the majority of skills they were looking for and the candidate gets additional experience to add to their CV – it's a meeting somewhere in the middle.

Set realistic timescales

It's hard to determine exactly when you'll find that next job, but know for sure that you will. Self-belief is critical and you must 'attack from the high ground' at all times, as I discussed in Chapter 1.

It's also important to set yourself realistic expectations based on what's happening out there in the real world. If you've just been made redundant are you likely to find a job in a week? A lot will depend on your industry and pay grade, but a week is a very short space of time.

If you set yourself a target of finding a job in a week and a week later you're still looking, how do you think you'll feel? Pretty rubbish I'd imagine, down on yourself, questioning your abilities and all that other unproductive stuff! Is feeling like this going to help you find a job, is it going to put you in the right mindset?

Well, no it isn't! So why set yourself unrealistic targets?

Instead, do your research. Ask professional recruiters, talk to the job centre, read your industry's press and work out how long people on average with your skills and abilities are taking to move in the market and make this your timescale, because it's more realistic!

You're not going to get it exactly right and set a timescale of three months and on the last day of month three find that dream job. Setting a realistic timescale helps maintain your positive mindset and also allows you to budget. Budgeting is important – remember, this is a business plan! Any redundancy pay off or savings account can run out quickly, so budgeting is important. If you're constantly worrying about money it can and will affect your mood and mindset and desperation to find a job will creep in and show up in communications with everyone you meet.

Mirroring your expenditure budget to a realistic timescale takes this pressure away. It takes the pressure off and enables you to stay calm, positive and focused on the task at hand of finding your next job. Identify a realistic timescale (let's assume it's three months) and work backwards to identify your daily expenditure budget. Crudely, this can be as simple as dividing your redundancy pay off by 90 to give you a daily allowance.

Remember that this is in no way an exact science, so building in a contingency is always a good idea, just in case it takes you a little bit longer.

Educate others

We all have significant others in our lives, Mum, Dad, Wife, Husband, Boyfriend, Girlfriend, Children, Cat or Dog! Are they aware of your situation; are they part of your plan?

I've interviewed many candidates over the years who in looking for a job are experiencing a difficult time at home. One such candidate, called Geoff, felt he was getting under his wife's feet; he felt guilty for being unemployed and felt his nearest and dearest was starting to resent him. I asked Geoff why he thought that was. He looked at me baffled and offered no answer.

It's because Geoff had not communicated his plan (he didn't actually have a plan when I met him but that's another story); he had not empowered his wife and wasn't bringing her along for the ride. She needed to be part of his journey as much as he needed her support, but the vacuum of non-communication bred resentment and guilt – not very empowering emotions when you are looking for a job!

The lesson here is to empower the people around you and in doing so empower them to help and support you in your job search. If they know you have a plan and are working to that plan, they are going to feel more positive about you finding a job and can also help you stick to the plan you have set out for yourself.

Write it down and be accountable

In my experience, unless you write something down it doesn't get done. Having decided on your plan to ensure the foundations stay firmly rooted to the ground, you must write it down. How you do this is up to you, but my advice is to take your realistic timescale and break it down into days and components (I'll expand more on this shortly). Once your plan is set you must stick to it and be accountable as there's no room for excuses.

If you've ever held a gym membership you've probably had this conversation with yourself:

"It's been a long day, I think I'll give the gym a miss tonight and go tomorrow." Tuesday comes. *"It's best I go to the gym tomorrow night now; I want to catch that documentary that's on later."* Wednesday, Thursday pass and Friday arrives. *"It's been a tough week; thank goodness it's the weekend. I'll start back at the gym on Monday for sure."*

Sound familiar? We've all done it! It's so easy to come up with reasons why you can't do things or should postpone doing them. It's so easy to make excuses and once you let yourself slip, it's a long hard slippery slope to doing nothing at all.

Rather than having the conversation with yourself every night, how much easier would it have been to bite the bullet and go to the gym on Monday? And, you know what, having gone on Monday and enjoyed yourself you probably would have gone Tuesday, Wednesday and Thursday – how great you would and could have felt for the weekend!

Make sure you communicate your plan to your significant others, give them a copy, stick it on the wall and look at it at the start and end of every day.

The power of rest

When I talk to jobseekers and ask them what they are doing to find a job they're keen to tell me about all the job boards they're surfing. As you'll see by reading the rest of this book, this is no longer enough, but the point in this chapter is that they don't know when to down tools.

The internet is accessible round the clock seven days a week and as such, so is the ability to surf the job boards. This is dangerous! If you worked 24/7, how productive would you be and how fed up of working would you become? I imagine you'd be very tired, pretty depressed and not a whole lot of use to anyone. The culture in many countries has moved to working long hours and long hours are perceived as doing a good job and being productive!

Remember Geoff? Well, no one could accuse Geoff of not trying; he was just doing the wrong things and too much of the wrong things. You see Geoff's plan by default (he didn't have a proper and well thought-out plan) was to search the job boards morning, noon and night. He was on them at the crack of dawn, at lunch and last thing before bed. He never left the house and conversations with his wife were an unwanted distraction from his computer. Geoff's life was job hunting. Nothing else mattered, he cared about little else and he was miserable. Geoff was miserable because he never took a break, he was at it 24/7, he rarely left the house and his relationship with his wife deteriorated as he didn't communicate properly.

All professional athletes know that rest is just as important as training. They exert their muscles, then rest to allow their muscles to repair and grow – that's how in simple terms they get bigger, faster and stronger!

Now the mind needs care and attention too – never taking a break is unproductive – yet so many jobseekers over work and then wonder why they underperform. This is one of the reasons why it's important to have a clearly defined plan. Know what you have to do today, do it, then once it's done forget it and rest as tomorrow is on its way.

Tick off actions once completed and psychologically you build a sense of achievement that yes, you did well today and furthered your quest to find that job. Focused effort with time off is far better than doing something all the time and trying to fit the rest of your life around it.

Ok, so now you understand the solid foundations needed for a successful job search and these should form the backbone of your business plan to find your next position.

Let's now look at the individual components of building the plan or put another way – let's break the plan into manageable bitesize chunks.

Think of a marathon runner, did they start out by getting up one day and thinking to themselves, I know let's run a marathon today? They may have done but I doubt it. More likely is that they built up to their end goal of running a marathon by breaking the task down into smaller chunks. Over a period of months they will have built up the distance run, factored in rest days and included other training, all leading to that ultimate goal of running the marathon.

With this in mind, let's look at the components of the business plan.

Components

Firstly, let's agree some ground rules. You can tweak these to suit your individual circumstances but not too much to defeat their importance.

The rules:

Get up early – Ever heard the phrase *"the early bird catches the worm"*? Getting up early and starting the day well puts you into a very positive state of mind.

Visualise – At the start of every day, remind yourself of your ultimate goal. Close your eyes and think about the company you want to work for and the job you want. Do this for at least five minutes and imagine how you will feel when you get the job offer and sign on the dotted line. You might feel silly doing this but trust me this daily reminder of what you are going after can have a huge effect – if you're still not convinced just type *'Anthony Robbins'* into Google.

Exercise every day – 'Healthy body, healthy mind', is something I'm sure you'll have heard, and again it's true. Whatever your level of fitness, some form of exercise, whether it's a brisk walk or an intensive gym session, builds your energy, mental alertness and keeps you happy. Whether you do this at the start or back end of the day is up to you – the important thing is that you do it. Over the years I've found what works for me – swimming in the morning before work always means I have a better day in the office. You just need to find what works for you!

Leave the house – Whatever you do, you must leave the house at least once a day, whatever the weather! Sitting indoors for an extended period of time will drive you crazy and will also make you depressed. Trust me, I've done it! If you're using the internet to research a company or to look at job boards, go to a coffee shop (most of them have free internet access these days) and get out of the house!

Break up the day – When I think about breaking up the day, I always think of the film starring Hugh Grant called *About a Boy*. Without going into detail, Hugh Grant is a single guy who doesn't work as he doesn't need to. He divides his day in to manageable chunks or units of time (half an hour) to stop himself getting bored. He spends one unit of time buying DVDs, two units having lunch and then another unit taking a stroll. The point is that he mixes things up to keep his interest and as a serious jobseeker you need to do this too.

The weekends are still the weekends – Treat the weekends as sacred and don't work! Don't check your inbox, surf the net or do anything remotely related to finding that next job. Instead, use this time for things you enjoy, your family, hobbies and interests.

Set your start and finish – If you're focused on finding that next job for more than seven and a half hours a day then you're doing too much. Do too much in one day and you'll get tired and fed up, so you are likely to do less tomorrow; so set and stick to your start and finish times. Outside of these hours don't do anything related to your job search – don't even talk about it! Instead, focus on the things you enjoy, as there's always tomorrow.

Just so you know, I followed these rules on my book writing days. Writing this book required extended periods of concentration and time at my desk, but when writing I always made time for exercise. I left the house at least once a day and I knew when I'd done enough for one day. Also, before I put fingers to keyboard I visualised this book selling in stores and walking in to buy a copy!

Below is an example of how to split your day to make best use of your time and to keep you engaged and motivated. The various activities are discussed throughout this book, so the ones I haven't covered yet I will get to later.

Example of a daily action plan

Time	Activity	Tick when completed
8.00 – 8.30am	Watch the news with breakfast and visualise your goal.	
8.30 – 9.00am	Check your inbox and respond to urgent emails.	
9.00 – 10.45am	Networking events/meetings.	
10.45 – 11.00am	Tea/coffee break.	
11.00 – 12.00pm	Telephone calls to follow up on applications/meetings.	
12.00 – 1.00pm	Target letters to businesses.	
1.00 – 2.00pm	Lunch and brisk walk to post letters.	
2.00 – 3.00pm	Work on online presence.	
3.00 – 3.15pm	Tea/coffee break.	
3.15 – 4.30pm	Review job boards and online applications.	
4.30 – 5.00pm	Catch up time to tie up any loose ends.	

Look carefully – what do you notice about this plan?

Think about the timing of certain activities – does anything jump out?

There are two things you should notice that are important to get right in your plan.

1. The day is set up to do the difficult things first. It's harder to get out to meetings and make telephone calls than it is to sit in front of your computer. The tougher to do things are done first to make sure they get done and everything after that is just a breeze.

2. Networking events and meetings are done first thing, as they get you out of the house. They get you engaging face to face with people and it's a great way to start the day.

Remember, your daily activity plan might look like this but it might be completely different. What's important is that you have a plan, and more important than that is that you stick to it. The aim every day is to tick the 'completed' box and there's no excuse for not doing so!

Carry it through

Let's be honest, we've all created plans, spent time chopping and changing things, rearranging and making everything look nice.

I used to do this at school all the time when it came to exam revision. I'd spend at least a couple of days devising my colour coordinated, all encompassing, master plan to get the grades I wanted.

I'd be very pleased with all my hard work and while I'd stick my plan proudly on the wall for all to see, that's the only sticking I'd do. You see I'd never stick to anything on the plan and did what I felt like doing at the time. I had no discipline and things would slip. If I let things slip once, they could slip a little more – I was kidding myself!

Now I'm not saying investing time in planning is a waste of time, clearly I'm not as this chapter is dedicated to the importance of planning. What I am saying however, is that creating a plan you don't follow is absolutely pointless!

We all think we can stick to a plan but that's because we are our own worst enemy. There is no better kidder than yourself, so a plan is not complete unless you've put three safety nets in place. These safety nets give you the best possible chance of sticking to your plan and achieving your goal.

They are:

1. Peer pressure

2. Measurement

3. Rewards.

Let's look at each in detail.

Peer pressure

If you tell someone you're going to do something, you're more likely to do it. But, if you've agreed to do something with someone else then you're almost certain to do it.

Let's look at a quick example. I leave work for the evening and tell my work colleague Martin that I'm off to the gym. I get in the car and on the way home I make up an excuse, change direction and drive home instead. The next day Martin asks, *"How was the gym?"* I feel a bit sheepish as I told him I was going, so I make up an excuse and it's on with the day.

But, what if I'd arranged to meet Martin at the gym to lift weights together? I'd have had to have turned up as we'd made an arrangement and also the session might have been easier as Martin would've been there to encourage, motivate and push me along.

Let me ask you a quick question – are you the only person out of work or looking for a job at this time? I can tell you with certainty that the answer is most definitely no! Even if you don't know someone else in a similar situation to you, they are likely to be everywhere you are going and doing lots of the things that you are doing (particularly if they've read this book). Teaming up with someone else is a great idea and can be mutually beneficial, motivating and rewarding and something you should be open to.

Measurement

Have you ever heard the expression, *'What gets measured gets done'*? Well this is so true! Even if you've allocated time in your daily plan for a particular action, it's easy to let this time slip by and complete very little. We all get distracted, but when we focus on a target we must hit and strive to exceed, it's amazing how distraction takes a back seat.

Take a look at the daily action plan below. It's the same one I presented earlier but with the added dimension of targets (highlighted by the use of italics) for a given action. There is also an extra column to record the number of actions successfully completed – by way of demonstration I've filled in the number as equivalent to target.

Example of a daily action plan with measurement

Time	Activity	Number	Tick when completed
8.00 - 8.30am	Watch the news with breakfast and visualise your goal.		
8.30 - 9.00am	Check inbox and respond to urgent emails.		
9.00 - 10.45am	Networking events or meetings (*target of 1 per day*).	1	
10.45 - 11.00am	Tea/coffee break.		
11.00 - 12.00pm	Telephone calls to follow up on applications/meetings (*target of 6 decision makers reached*).	6	
12.00 - 1.00pm	Target letters to businesses (*target of 3 sent*).	3	
1.00 - 2.00pm	Lunch and brisk walk to post letters.		
2.00 - 3.00pm	Work on online presence (*target on LinkedIn of 5 new connections and 3 posts in relevant groups*).	5 & 3	
3.00 - 3.15pm	Tea/coffee break.		
3.15 - 4.30pm	Review job boards and online applications (*target of 3 applications*).	3	
4.30 - 5.00pm	Catch up time to tie up any loose ends.		

Completing this on a daily basis and calculating a total for the week gives you a clear picture of your activity levels and enables you to identify some interesting trends that show your level of expertise.

As an example take a look at the following table which records the number of meetings arranged and their source over a four-week period.

Meetings resulting from:	Letters sent	Networking events	LinkedIn contacts	Total
Week 1	1	2	3	6
Week 2	4	5	5	14
Week 3	2	2	2	6
Week 4	1	2	4	7
Total	8	11	14	33

The table is fairly simplistic but highlights some interesting things that unless you'd measured you would never have known.

Firstly, in week 2, productivity went through the roof compared to other weeks in the month. Why was this and what can be learned? Were you doing something different that due to the results you should be doing consistently?

Secondly, LinkedIn has generated the most meetings. Is this an area you should be focussing more on and allocating more time to?

Knowledge is power as they say and some measure of performance not only helps to channel your energies in the right direction, it also keeps you motivated. Simple measurements can be very useful, but whatever you do, make sure you avoid over analysis (often called paralysis by analysis) as this will only confuse and get in the way of what you are trying to achieve!

Rewards

As part of our growth strategy in my company, all consultants are required to make outgoing business development calls. Not everyone likes doing this; it can be hard to get to the decision maker and you don't always get the response you'd hoped for or expected.

To encourage the team to make more calls, we introduced a rewards system. We also encouraged our consultants to call in groups (this goes back to my point on peer pressure). Whoever speaks to the most decision makers in an hour wins a bottle of wine or similar – this has had a dramatic effect on performance. The promise of a reward, no matter how small, gets things moving and gets people motivated.

As part of completing your plan, make sure you reward yourself. It can be something silly – if you hit your target number of calls or letters in the allocated time slot then maybe you get a chocolate biscuit with your tea or coffee – if you don't you get nothing! It's not the value of the prize, it's the recognition that you've hit the number and earned your reward that's important – try it and you'll see!

Summary

Creating a plan and following it through can be daunting, especially if you've never done it before. If planning fills you with fear because you've never done it before then good, because others will feel the fear too which will stop them taking the action you are committed to take to find that next job! Take planning and sticking to the plan seriously, but don't take yourself too seriously. Make sure you have fun with it, as what's fun gets done and what's not gets shot!

EFFECTIVE
NETWORKING

I n Chapter 1, I discussed 'attacking from the high ground' – setting the scene for battle to guarantee victory. Imagine if you could avoid engaging the enemy directly and use other people to fight your battles for you – how good would that be? I watched the film *Gladiator* the other night, starring Russell Crowe, where the opening scenes are of a brutal battle in a forest. Russell Crowe's character, Maximus Decimus Meridius, is fully embroiled in the blood and guts while Caesar watches comfortably and safely from afar. Who would you rather be? I'll get back to this later!

We all have an idea or a notion as to what networking is and what it entails. For many people it's the thing they know they should be doing but the thing they dread doing the most – so guess what... they don't do it! In life we all lean towards what we like and what makes us comfortable. If it's raining or cold, we are great at convincing ourselves that going out for our regular morning run is a bad idea and that we'd be much better staying in our nice warm bed.

The truth is that the harder or more uncomfortable something appears to be, then often it's the thing that's most important and the thing we expend energy on to avoid at all costs. What if we accepted that it's tough to do and directed that energy in a positive way to make it work for us? This all starts with understanding.

So what is networking? Well, my dictionary defines it as *'a supportive system of sharing information and services among individuals and groups having a common interest'*. It goes on to say that networks are *'formed to provide mutual assistance'*.

Yes, these are all true and further on in the definition my dictionary pinpoints *'to cultivate people who can be helpful to one professionally, especially in finding employment or moving to a higher position'*. This latter definition gets to the heart of what networking needs to be for you; the jobseeker looking for that next move.

We need to be clear on one other point before we progress and that is that recruitment gets done face to face. There are some exceptions to this rule where individuals are hired solely on their technical skills, which can and often happens in the IT sector. This is the exception rather than the rule. When people are hiring, they are not only thinking about skills; they are also thinking about whether they can spend their working week with this person and whether or not they will get on with the rest of the team.

In the next chapter, I discuss using the internet, and specifically social media, to raise your profile to find that next role. I also will explain how this medium can be used for networking.

The ordering of Chapters 5 and 6 is no accident – it's deliberate! Many jobseekers I meet think that all networking can be done on the internet in remote cyberspace – this is a myth. In this chapter I discuss the end goal, i.e. face to face engagements and in the next chapter I explain how you can use the internet to help generate these.

As you will find out, using the internet to develop relationships only goes so far. It helps pinpoint fairly accurately who you should be in communication with, but online communication is always a precursor to a face to face meeting where the real relationship building gets done. Please remember this as you read on – it's important.

To network effectively you need to first ask yourself the following questions:

- Who?
- Where?
- How?
- How often?

If this seems confusing and a little daunting, don't worry! I'm going to walk you through each stage and by the end of this chapter you will have all the tools you need to start EFFECTIVE networking. That word EFFECTIVE is very important.

I've been to more networking events than I can shake a stick at and at pretty much all of these events you find two extremes of people, namely:

1. Mr or Mrs **ALSIC**

2. Mr or Mrs **HAMBUC**

Before you decide if you fall in to either camp, let's look at these two in more detail.

Mr or Mrs ALSIC or more specifically **A**rrive **L**ate and **S**tand **I**n the **C**orner, do as described.

They arrive late, particularly if the event involves a formal presentation or similar. Their mission is to avoid the standing around beforehand at all costs, because this might actually mean talking to someone they don't know and have never met before. They arrive as the formal event begins and leave as soon as it ends – they've missed the point completely but convince themselves that it's been a morning, afternoon or evening well spent – how deluded!

Sometimes Mr and Mrs ALSIC are a little more adventurous, so let's not give up on them just yet. They sometimes go to events together, yes together! Now boosted by the presence of their partner in crime (and yes it is a crime and a wasted opportunity how they go about things) they arrive a little earlier and stand in the corner talking to each other over coffee. They might even stick around at the end for a sandwich or biscuit and again take up their position in the corner talking to one another. They go home feeling good because this time they stayed a little longer and actually got something to eat and drink. Three words spring to mind here and they are – WASTE OF TIME!

Ok, we've heard enough from Mr and Mrs ALSIC, let's catch up with Mr or Mrs HAMBUC or, more specifically, **H**and out **A**ll **M**y **BU**siness **C**ards, to as many people as possible.

Mr and Mrs HAMBUC work hard, there's no doubt about it. I usually get tired just watching them. They arrive early and stay at the end, they are often the first to arrive and the last to leave – you have to give them credit for trying – indeed that's what they are – very trying!

You have to be quick to spot them as they move fast and don't hang around. You'll know if you've met them as they'll come up to you and say:

"Hi, my name's John, John HAMBUC – do you have a business card please?"

You duly hand over your business card. They then say:

"Thank you – here's my card. Nice to meet you."

If they're not too pushed for time they might even shake your hand on arrival and departure but if it's a packed event there'll be no time for that – they've got too many people to get round!

And that's what they do, over and over again until they've got round the whole room and have handed out, as well as collected, as many business cards as possible. I often wish I could rig up a video camera, film the event and then play it back at speed – you'd see Mr and Mrs HAMBUC cover every square inch of the room and talk at, not to, everyone.

Their strategy works even better when they go along together. They have double the resources, so they can hit everyone in half the time, or at a bigger event twice as many people in the same time. They then pat themselves on the back and head home – they're pleased as it's been another great event and the measure of their success is how many business cards they've collected. You might hear them say to one another, *"Well that one wasn't as good as last week, we got 50 business cards then but only 34 today – we'll have to try harder next time!"*

Three words again spring to mind – CRAZY MAD FOOLS! Let me ask you a question – what do you think they do with all those business cards? The answer is probably nothing… that is unless you count filing them in a desk drawer at home something!

But why do they do nothing with them, after all they've gone to so much effort? There are two reasons for this:

1. They don't know what to do.
2. They have too many to do anything with.

If you can identify with Mr and Mrs ALSIC or Mr and Mrs HAMBUC don't worry, I suspect that many people reading this book will do – as they say, you are not alone! Recognising who you are currently is the first step on the road to changing your actions and behaviours to generate success from networking.

The ALSICs and HAMBUCs are not just characters I've created; they are real people that attend networking events every day. The next time you attend such an event see if you can spot them. If you can, you already have a deeper understanding of how to network successfully, as you recognise what not to do.

It's fairly obvious stuff isn't it – to network effectively you must engage with people you don't know (unlike the ALSICs) and you need to generate a deeper relationship than just a quick *"Hello"* and exchange of business cards, unless your name is HAMBUC.

But if it's so obvious then why do so many people fall into this trap?

There are two reasons:

1. They don't have a plan.
2. They have no measure of success.

I'm sure you've heard it said before that if you don't plan then you plan to fail (I covered this in the previous chapter) – well, it's very true. Linked to this is that without a plan you have no valuable measure of performance, as you have nothing to measure against.

So, we've set the scene and understand what not to do, so now let's get in to the meat of the subject. Hopefully you remember that I said earlier that you need to have thought about, and more than that, actually have planned:

- Who?
- Where?
- How?
- How often?

Let's look at each one in detail.

Who?

Think about who can find you or help you find your next job. I don't know your industry, so this is something you really need to think about for yourself. It's not rocket science and the answer will to some extent be staring you in the face – you've perhaps just not thought about it before. Don't worry, these people are common to all industry sectors – they exist everywhere and the good news is that they will be keen to talk to you. Yes, I'll say it again – THEY WILL BE KEEN TO TALK TO YOU!

I call these people *'marketmakers'* – not sure if this is a word or not or whether it's grammatically correct – I don't really care – it's functional and describes what these people do – they make things happen for you.

At a networking event, what are the chances of you bumping into someone who is at this time, right now looking to hire someone with your skill set? I'm not one for statistics but I can tell you it's pretty slim. The more networking events you go to and the more specific these events are to your industry then of course the odds go up, but there's still only a slim chance. Also, think about all those events you'll have to go to – how much time do you have?

Personally, I like to be rewarded for my time and effort and you need to start thinking like this too. If it doesn't potentially pay (not just in the financial sense) then don't do it. This approach might suit Mr and Mrs HAMBUC but it doesn't suit us. So forget trying to meet someone who is going to be in a position to offer you the job you are looking for – just plain forget it!

Now that you've forgotten it this should relieve some pressure as you are no longer going to a networking event to meet someone who can offer you a job. You are going to meet marketmakers who can, and given the right circumstances will, introduce you to people that can offer you a job. The last time you had a leak in your house and needed a plumber, what did you do? You might have gone straight to a directory listing or done an internet search, but I suspect you probably asked a few people you if they could recommend someone. Why do this, why not just call the first random number that comes up in a list of plumbers?

The answer is that people are all a little risk averse. At the start of this chapter I talked about being comfortable. We all like to be comfortable and we'll do anything in our power to make sure we stay that way.

If I know Tom across the road has had some plumbing work done and that ABC Plumbing has done a good job, I'm far more likely to call ABC Plumbing ahead of any other plumber and that's because they have a track record of doing a good job – not for me personally, but for someone I trust. It's the same in business and it's the same in employment.

I have been a professional recruiter for many years and what I can tell you is that there are three levels of conversation that someone looking to hire will have. My specialism is in the accounting and finance sector, which my example below illustrates, but the principle transcends all industries.

So let's look at that example.

Michael Dock is Managing Director of his own business – let's call him MD for short. Well, MD has a problem, his Finance Director, Freddie Diligent or FD for short, has just left the company and he needs to replace him. So what does he do? Well, he has three conversations and here they are:

Conversation 1

MD asks his peer group. These are people he knows well. They are likely to be long standing friends or individuals he knows through business and has developed a respect for or a personal friendship with.

He phones them up and says, *"My FD is moving on, do you know anyone that might be able to replace him, or can you recommend anyone I should be speaking to?"*

He'll have a few conversations like this and may or may not get somewhere. When his personal trusted network is exhausted he moves on to Conversation 2.

Conversation 2

In his business MD has professional advisors. They are not quite in the inner circle, they're not friends or business associates who have become friends – nevertheless they are people he respects and whose opinion he values.

He phones up his Auditor and says, *"My FD is moving on, do you know anyone that might be able to replace him, or can you recommend anyone I should be speaking to?"*

Now, his Auditor is a professionally qualified accountant, so is likely to have contacts in the industry. His network is likely to be bigger and more specific to MD's needs.

MD is very likely to have success in finding his next FD through conversations like this. Note that he is still looking for a recommendation – he still wants that comfort.

If he has no luck, then he will move on to Conversation 3.

Conversation 3

Finally, if MD gets nowhere with Conversations 1 and 2, he is down to his last conversation or better put, conversations! He talks to a newspaper, publication and/or job board about placing an advertisement. Alternatively, it could be with a recruitment business about engaging their services to find his next FD.

There are two massively important points to understand here, so please read the following over and over again until it hits home.

1. Both of the options in Conversation 3 cost MD money; Conversations 1 and 2 cost nothing.

2. Conversation 3 comes with less comfort – there is no personal recommendation. Although there is likely to be a professional

recommendation from a recruiter it is not as strong as those sourced from Conversations 1 and 2.

If Conversations 1, 2 and 3 were ponds, which pond or ponds do you think MD would prefer to fish in? That's right – ponds 1 and 2 – it's free and there is a stronger recommendation. But, in which pond do most jobseekers place themselves? They swim in pond 3 because it's easier, it takes them less time and they can stay well and truly in their comfort zone. But there's a big problem, as pond 3 is where the majority of fish (other jobseekers) swim. Not only is it the most competitive pond to swim in, it's where MD would prefer not to fish!

This should be obvious but time and time again, when I meet or interview jobseekers and ask them what they are doing to find their next job tell me that they are swimming in pond 3. When I ask them what else they are doing they look at me blankly!

This is one of the main reasons I decided to write this book.

So what does all of this have to do with networking I hear you ask? After all, this chapter is titled 'effective networking' isn't it? That's because networking takes place in ponds 1 and 2. Jobseekers who network and network effectively (more on this later) put themselves right at the heart of ponds 1 and 2, with less fish and right where MD, or his equivalent, prefers to go fishing – it's that simple!

So let's get back to 'who' and to the marketmakers. The marketmakers are the people that MD in the example above talked to in Conversations 1 and 2. Although they exist in pond 1, as a jobseeker looking to network you are more likely to meet those swimming in pond 2. You've met these people many times already; you may have even spoken to them or they may have just swam right by. But how do you know who they are and how can you best identify them? This is where the planning comes in.

Let's do a quick exercise – take a moment and grab a piece of paper and a pen.

In the centre of the page draw a circle and write the word TARGET. Next, draw slightly smaller circles surrounding the TARGET circle and connect them with a line – start with three or four and leave them blank for the moment.

Now comes the hard work and the brainstorming – I promise you that you know the answers already, but it might prove difficult as you've never thought this way. Remember riding a bike for the first time? Difficult wasn't it – no doubt you fell off a few times? Remember everything is difficult the first few times you do it so don't be deterred.

You need to think about who MD in your industry would talk to in Conversation 2. Before you do this though, you need take a step back and work out who MD is in your industry, i.e. who will be the person recruiting the job you are looking to find and to hire the skill set you possess. I can't answer this for you – you will know your job and sector far better than I. If you are in sales it's likely to be a Sales Director, if you are in administration it could be an Office Manager – you will know who it is for your industry. If you can't identify these people straightaway think about who you last reported to – what was their job title and area of responsibility?

The TARGET is your MD. Once you know who MD is you can start to brainstorm who he or she would have Conversation 2 with.

Remember those three or four blank circles? Now's the time to fill them in, with those people whom your MD may speak to during Conversation 2. To help you I've done it below for MD who is looking to recruit his FD.

So in my example above, MD is likely to have Conversation 2 with his:

- Auditor/Accountant

- Solicitor/Lawyer

- Business Coach

- Sales/Business Development Director

What do all of the above have in common? Can you spot it?

Well, all of the above as part of their role, will be responsible for developing their own networks to win business for their respective organisations.

When doing this exercise AIM HIGH. Your TARGET and also your target's marketmakers must be decision makers. They must be the people in their business who have the authority and responsibility for making decisions.

Furthermore, the more senior an individual becomes in a business, then in my experience the more likely they are to be involved in driving sales for their business – but what does all this mean?

It means that these people are likely to be at the same networking events as you and that they have a level of authority and standing that means they are likely to be engaged in Conversation 2 by your target.

Even more importantly, if you can identify and build a relationship with these marketmakers, they might just introduce you to your target. Remember, they do business with your target so if they can help your target with his or her recruitment problem then they surely will – it makes them look good!

Because these marketmakers are in the business of networking and doing business, they will have multiple business relationships.

Remember Mr and Mrs HAMBUC whose aim it was to hand out 50 or so business cards at every networking event? Maintaining a strong relationship with 50 people is extremely difficult, if not impossible, and most definitely far too time consuming.

I'm a marketmaker and have roughly 15 key relationships that bring me over 50% of my business. Don't get me wrong, it's taken me time to identify and build those relationships – it doesn't just happen overnight. Could I handle more? Possibly, but it could be at the detriment of my already established relationships that are already working hard for me and paying off.

Remember *Gladiator* and Maximus Decimus Meridius? Well, I'd much prefer the role of Caesar!

You may have heard of the theory of compound interest. Interest in a bank earns interest and this compounds as you then earn interest on your interest and so on and so on. Well, there something I like to call compound networking.

Take a look at the diagram below.

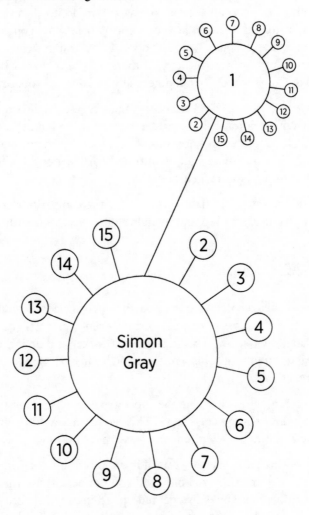

Each of my marketmakers will in turn have 15 or so key relationships of their own. Each of their relationships could potentially be with my target. Therefore, by having 15 quality relationships with marketmakers I am effectively making indirect contact with an additional 225 people who may be targets or who could introduce me to my target – this is how I generate business.

Ever heard the expression that business is done on the golf course? Well it is, but you don't need to play golf to do it – I can't hit golf balls for toffee! Business is done informally and the golf course is one example of a place where it's done. Conversations you have and relationships built with the right marketmakers in your industry lead to Conversation 2 and, potentially, to your next opportunity.

Please understand that I'm not saying disregard job boards and to avoid conversations with recruiters – as I am one I'm definitely not saying this! Recruiters know lots of people and are some of the best networkers out there but, as outlined earlier, not all of the job opportunities land at their door.

What I am saying, is that to get ahead of the competition you need to think outside the box and swim in a different, less crowded pond.

Where?

So we've talked about who you should be getting close to, but where to do it? There are so many networking events; in fact it's quite easy nowadays to become a professional networker and do it morning, noon and night, but this won't get you your next job – a targeted approach will.

As human beings we have the capacity to produce energy. Food goes in and energy comes out. This energy allows us to breathe, move and interact – without energy we have nothing.

Networking takes energy – lots of it and more still. It's tiring and if you do it all the time, not only will you not perform to the best of your ability, but you'll also get fed up. To network effectively you need to be in the right state of mind, alert, confident (without being arrogant) and exuding energy – so don't do too much!

If you're not going to do too much, then you best make sure you go to the right events. I've been to hundreds of networking events, some great and some terrible – this experience has given me an insight as to what's important and which ones to go to.

To help me decide which events to go to I put together a checklist which I will share with you now – I call it my 'should I stay or should I go?' Following it has saved me lots of wasted hours, which I've put to far better use. As a jobseeker you have a fulltime job and that's finding your next job, so an hour saved here and spent productively elsewhere will lead to better results – this is how you need to think.

Networking Event Checklist – 'should I stay or should I go'?

Before attending a networking event I check the following:

1. It needs to be held within my geographical area – the area that I am looking to find a job.

Why? Well, if it's in my locality or target geography it will attract marketmakers from my locality or target geography with useful contacts and knowledge. The exception would be for an industry specific conference that draws a wider audience. This may also be worth attending, but appreciate that the geographical concentration of the audience will be diluted. If you have national and indeed international flexibility then this is less of a concern, but the cost of investment (petrol, train fares, hotel and entry fee) versus any to potential reward will be something to take in to account.

2. The event must have an educational element, e.g. a guest speaker talking on a particular subject relevant to my industry or something that I have an interest in.

Why? If I'm investing my time I need to be certain I'm going to derive some benefit along the way or let's face it what's the point? You must expect that at some events you won't meet a marketmaker worth building a relationship with – expect it and don't be phased by it – that's just the way of the world.

However, if I go to an event that teaches me something, and from which I derive some intellectual benefit, then it has been time well spent. This also widens my scope of knowledge when entering in to dialogue with future marketmakers – the wider my knowledge then the more easily I can converse on a range of topics.

Another important reason to go to an event that has a guest speaker or similar is that it breaks the ice. Other people attending will be there because they also find the topic interesting, so you have something in common already. It's very easy on arrival over coffee to say to someone, *"I'm really looking forward to hearing James speak today... have you heard him talk on this subject before?"* Bingo – you're in a conversation and you didn't even have to try!

3.   Have I been before and is it worth going again?

Why? Save yourself some time – if you've been to an event before that wasn't so good is it worth going again? Chances are that unless something has radically changed in terms of organisation and format then it's probably not worth going.

And that's it – only three things to consider. If you stick to this checklist you'll be consistent in the quality of networking events you go to. These questions are designed to protect your energy and time – please remember that.

So, how do you find events that you might want to go to? It's common sense really and once you get going you'll start to find that all sorts of people invite you to all sorts of events. This is a nice problem to have, but is where my checklist comes in very handy.

Places to find the right events to attend:

- Look in publications relevant to your industry – there is a good chance the right marketmakers will also be attending.

- Internet – I talk in the next chapter about LinkedIn and will cover 'Groups' and 'Events' – these are great places to find out details of relevant events.

- Word of mouth – This, in my opinion, is by far the best way to find out where to go and it's also a great way to engage in dialogue. It also provides you with another topic of conversation! By default, this way of uncovering networking events also comes with a built in recommendation. People are unlikely to recommend a bad networking event to you, as they know that there's a really good chance that they'll run into you again!

Please remember that just because an event is not specifically badged as a networking event, doesn't mean it isn't. Anywhere where people gather with a common interest can be a networking opportunity and sometimes the most unlikely of situations lead to the best results. It really boils down to asking questions and taking an interest in people, but more on that shortly.

How many and how much?

Being out of work and spending too much time at home surfing job boards is no way to find work. Over time it can also eat away at your confidence and it will mean that you are not practicing your communication skills that you'll need at every stage of a recruitment process.

How many networking events you attend per week depends on the quality of those events. I can't sit here and say you must go to two or three a week because I don't know your industry. What I would say though, is that if you're not attending at least one event per week something is wrong – you need this personal interaction to stay positive and sharp.

Ultimately, you need to build networking into your jobseeker business plan; it's a tool in your toolbox and you need to use it.

The other consideration is cost – some events (and some of the best ones) are free. If you're out of work and not drawing a wage or salary then this is an important consideration. Keep a log of what you are spending and make sure this doesn't escalate out of control. Remember, it's not only your time that you are giving to attend, for the paid events it's also the contents of your wallet!

How?

Now let's get into the nitty gritty of how to do it – how to strike up that conversation, how to be liked, how to start off those relationships that if nourished and managed well can be so fruitful in your job search.

The first thing to point out is that this isn't rocket science. It's all just common sense, but the irony is that people are put off this important aspect of finding their next job because they think to be good at it you have to do something special or be someone special.

Stop right there...!

Remember, you are someone special; you have skills, experience and are an expert in your field. As long as you know more about a subject than the person you are talking to, in their eyes you are an expert.

For example, once you've finished this book you will have an arsenal of skills to share with people on finding a job in a difficult market – that makes you an expert. So with these thoughts in your head, here are my tips for successful networking once you're there and in the thick of it – but to emphasise the point again, it's just plain old common sense.

I can pretty much guarantee you that everyone at the event is in the same boat, i.e. they're all worried about what it will be like and who to talk to. Knowing this should empower you, as people will be just as keen to talk to you as you are to them.

Common Sense Tips for Successful Networking

Get there early!

One of the reasons people avoid networking events is because they don't like walking into a room full of people they don't know and worse still, having to walk up to someone they don't know and engage in conversation.

That's so easy to resolve – just get there early or better still, be first! Ironically people, including Mr and Mrs ALSIC, get there late because they are scared of the whole prospect of networking. They could transform their results and knockout the fear by getting there early.

This is a great strategy that has multiple wins attached to it, including:

- There's no queue for the coffee or biscuits! Also, in all seriousness with less people there you're less likely to drop hot coffee over someone – never a good reason to be remembered, trust me!

- You get to speak and to build a relationship with the organiser. By definition the organiser of events is usually an excellent marketmaker, so get to know them. They can also introduce you to other attendees as they arrive and these other attendees will be keen to talk to you, as if you're talking to the organiser then you must be important.

- Once you've built a relationship with the organiser, he or she is more likely to let you see a copy of the delegate list or the sign-in sheet in advance. Being the first or one of the first there, you have a chance to take a good look at it. Remember that all-important concept of planning; you have a unique opportunity to identify key people that you want to speak to. I've been to a networking event before where someone I'd never met before came up to me and said something along the lines of, *"Hi Simon, I saw your name on the delegate list and was really keen to come and speak to you...!"* This is not me being big-headed, it happened – so, do you think I was keen to speak to this person? Too right I was. I was flattered and also very intrigued. This strategy worked on me, so use it!

- As you're already talking to the organiser this is a great opportunity to ask them who they recommend you speak with and better still ask then to introduce you!

Become the pourer!

"Pardon?", I hear you say, *"What is he on about now?!"* Seriously, standing next to the tea and coffee can be a fantastic place to position yourself.

Standing by the drinks means that you will catch people as they enter the room, before they are engaged in conversation with someone else. It also gives you the opportunity to spot your targets from the delegate list as they arrive.

Please note, I'm not saying pour everyone a drink. What I am saying is that it's a good place to hang out to spot the people you want to speak to. Also, you're unlikely to be left on your own for too long as people naturally gravitate to refreshments – after all, we're human aren't we?

I've used this strategy many times with great success – it's so simple but effective.

Don't try too hard!

It's very easy to think, goodness me, I'm at a networking event, I've got to let people know what I can do as soon as possible.

WRONG – this is one sure way to be left stood on your own in the corner of the room – your surname isn't HAMBUC is it?

We all like to talk about ourselves – fact! Giving people the opportunity to talk about themselves first has power. It puts them at ease and they will feel comfortable in your company.

Also, remember that we're born with two ears and one mouth – well there's a reason for this. In my experience of networking, good listeners have more success than good talkers. By listening we get to find out about the person we are talking to. Add in some carefully placed questions and you start to qualify them as a potential marketmaker or not.

Once initial introductions have been made examples of good open questions include:

- *"So, what are you currently working on in your business?"*

- *"What are some of the challenges you are facing at the moment?"*

I've included only a couple of examples here on purpose. This book is not designed to turn out clones, but to get you, as a jobseeker, to think differently and explore new ideas – so please do that, be creative, inventive and most importantly have fun, enjoy the experience and watch yourself grow.

Be patient – at some point in the conversation they will naturally ask what it is you do. You've not forced this upon them, they've asked you and this is the better way to play the game. Be careful, as this is the point that all the hard work you've done so far can be undone.

Let's look at an example. I'm at a networking event and am chatting to Susan. After a little while Susan asks:

"So Simon, what do you do for a living?"

Without thinking I reply:

"I'm a Director of a recruitment company called Cherry Professional Limited – we recruit finance and office support staff."

And that is where the conversation ends. Susan may have no interest in recruitment let alone finance and there are probably a handful of other recruitment people in the room that will say something very similar when asked the question.

Have I said anything memorable? Have I sparked her interest? Have I differentiated myself in any way? The answer is one big fat NO! So what could I have done differently?

Ever heard the saying – *"sell the sizzle not the sausage"*? Well this holds true here and in many other aspects of life!

Let's try again.

Susan – *"So Simon, what do you do for a living?"*

Me – *"I shape people's careers and help them find the opportunities they are looking for. At the moment though I'm taking a little time out to write a book to empower jobseekers to find their next position."*

Thoughts…?

This second way of answering the question is much more powerful. It's far more interesting, memorable and more importantly it prompts Susan to ask me a follow up question – it keeps the conversation flowing.

As a jobseeker, whether you are in or out of work you need to sell your sizzle in a similar way. I can't tell you what to say as it's your industry and your experience, but the principles are the same.

You can add in the line… *"but at the moment I'm considering other opportunities"*. This is a very subtle way of telling someone you are in the market for a job and is likely to prompt a follow on question – it keeps the conversation going.

One surefire way to send the person you are talking to off to the other side of the room is to tell them you are looking for a job and are here to meet people who can help you find one – NO, NO, NO and NO again – remember, don't try too hard!

What's in it for them?

We as humans want to know what's in it for us.

People you meet at networking events will be qualifying you just as much as you are qualifying them. As I've discussed you need to be engaging and interested (in them) and you should never ever try and sell your skills.

So, as the conversation continues and you've established that they have the potential to be a marketmaker, how do you ensure you've answered the question, *'What's in it for them?'* Make no mistake, you need to answer this question, even if they don't ask it – the fact that they will be thinking it is enough.

So why are you there? Stupid question, right? It's to network! Well, the person you're talking to is very likely to be there for the same reason. You are interested in their contacts and networks as a marketmaker and they will be interested in yours.

You need to let them know you have something they want, i.e. a network that they might be interested in. Even if you don't think you have a network, I promise you that you do. If you know someone other than yourself then you have a network. Even if your network isn't as big as the person's who you are talking to, it doesn't matter. Haven't you heard that size doesn't matter? It's what you do with it that counts!

However, one thing you never do is give your network up to someone you've just met (I'll talk more about this shortly). Why would you and why should you? What you can do though is hint about your contact base, in order to generate interest. What you're looking to achieve is a coffee away from the networking event you're currently at, just the two of you, to build a deeper understanding of how you can help each other.

The conversation should go something like this:

Me – *"So Susan, what kind of people are you looking to connect with to expand your network?"*

Susan – *"Well, I'm keen to meet up with people who have expertise in social media."*

Me – *"I see. Well I've ran in to a few people like that recently – you know, we should grab a coffee some time and have a chat about how we can help each other."*

Susan – *"That sounds good, let's exchange contact details and get something in the diary."*

It's that easy – I know because I have done it time and time again and you can do it too.

I now have a meeting in the diary, a meeting at which Susan and I can start to build an understanding of how, as marketmakers, we can help each other going forwards.

Trust me – you don't need many people like Susan looking out for you to help you find your next job. This is the smart way to network, it's painless, planned, targeted, productive and most of all it actually works!

How often?

How often here isn't how often you should attend a networking event – I've already covered this. What I'm talking about here is how often you should engage with your marketmakers to maximise leverage from those relationships in which you are investing your time and energy.

Have you ever recommended someone you've only met briefly to someone else you know well and who trusts you? If you have, how did it turn out? You may have been lucky, but often recommending or referring people you don't know can be a recipe for disaster.

Let's take a quick example.

MD calls me and says that his Sales Director is leaving this time (his business appears to have a high staff turnover, but that's another issue) and asks in a Conversation 2 if I can recommend anyone he can talk to. It just so happens that I met a Sales Director at a networking event the other week. I want to help MD as we have a good relationship that has been built up over many years, so racking my brains for the name of the lady I met I tell him I'll get back to him.

Back at home I check my wallet and pull out Mrs HAMBUC's business card that she kindly thrust upon me and guess what, she's the Sales Director. I call MD and pass on Mrs HAMBUC's details and MD gets in touch with her.

I don't hear from MD for a few weeks, which is unusual, as we tend to meet up on a fortnightly basis – I decide to call him.

I finally get through and in conversation I ask how he got on with Mrs HAMBUC. He dodges the question so I probe a bit deeper – finally he tells me that the meeting was a disaster, she turned up late, hadn't prepared and appeared to know very little about sales. MD wasted an hour of his time on this meeting but that's not the big cost – the big cost here is the damage to my reputation.

I put my professional integrity on the line in recommending Mrs HAMBUC without fully qualifying who I was recommending to a trusted contact. MD lost a little respect, lost a little trust and he only told me because I pushed him to – the damage took an hour and might take months or years to repair.

This is an example, but back in the real world I'm often asked for recommendations but NEVER, NEVER EVER recommend someone I am not 100% confident in.

But how can I gain confidence with someone I've met at a networking event so that I am in a position to recommend him or her?

There are three ways:

1. Time

2. Experience

3. Confirmation.

Time and experience go hand in hand. The more often I meet someone the more I get to know them and the more I get to understand their skills, capabilities and ethics – I get a feel for them and what makes them tick!

There is no substitute for time and experience – it requires investment from both sides but the payoffs can be big! This is why meetings with marketmakers like Susan are so important.

It's also a good idea to meet people in different surroundings and at different times – you get a better perspective as to who they are and what they are all about. We can all be one person at work but what are we like after hours?

The third way to gain confidence is what I like to call confirmation and this can lead to a quicker conversion time of someone you've met to someone you'd recommend.

But how does someone get confirmation? They think, or ask directly (or in a round about way), *"Who do you know that I know?"*

A common icebreaker when you meet someone new (that is once you've got past the weather) is, *"In your line of work I guess you must know...?"* or, *"Do you know...?"* The reason these questions are asked is to gain common ground quickly – another way to think of it is two islands joined by a ferry of commonality, which is someone known to both.

There is no exact formula as to how many meetings you should have before you can truly call someone a marketmaker, where you are in a position to recommend them and vice versa. The timing between the two of you might be slightly different too, but you won't know that. All you know is how confident you are and whether it's time for you to start recommending and introducing. When the time's right for you then the time is right for you.

Ever heard the phrase, *"What goes around comes around"*? When you're ready, make that recommendation and see what comes back – you might just be surprised!

The online 'YOU'

I f you don't exist in cyberspace you don't exist at all – just ask the youth of today. It's never been more important to have an online presence as another tool in your armoury and part of your strategy to find your next job.

Remember 'You' from the Introduction? That's 'You' or better put:

Yell – Out – Uniqueness!

Well, the opportunity to be unique and gain recognition online to get ahead in the job market is readily available to anyone.

Before we get into the detail, let's look at how things have changed in recent times. Indeed, the environment in which to find a job is constantly changing; it rarely changes overnight, but just as that extra indulgence on a regular basis leads to that unwanted pot belly, it will change over time.

Back in 1995, I graduated from university and decided, as many people do before starting work, to go and have a life experience and to travel the world. A group of us decided to travel down the East Coast of Australia and to meet up at various stops along the way to exchange traveller stories over the odd beer or two. But, as we were travelling in groups of two or three and all starting out at different times from different places how could we arrange to meet up? Big problem, as back in 1995 very few people had mobile phones, especially not poor students. Even if they had been readily available at a reasonable price, they would have been far too big to pack into a rucksack. Similarly, internet access – more specifically email – was not readily accessible. I didn't have my first Hotmail account until many years later.

In those days, communication involved something called Poste Restante, a service where a Post Office holds a letter for you until you pick it up. My friends could write to me at any Post Office and likewise I could do the same. If I wanted to meet Nick in Brisbane I wrote to him at Poste Restante Brisbane to let him know where I was staying in the hope he would pick up his letter and turn up at my hostel! The communication process was slow, unreliable and quite frankly, very hit and miss!

So what does all this travelling talk have to do with recruitment and what lessons does it hold for the jobseeker?

There are two key points:

1.   Things have become much faster.

2.   Things have become much easier.

Let me explain.

Most people nowadays have a mobile phone, email address and broadband. For me to get in contact with someone is easy. If I have their email address I can communicate with them instantaneously. As soon as I press the send button it arrives in their inbox and I can even select to receive a delivery confirmation. Sure, I might need to wait for a response as they may not read it straightaway (if at all) but I can even monitor this by setting a read notification.

With messenger services and online chat facilities I can even communicate with someone in real time. I no longer need to wait for a response as I do with email, as I can see if someone is currently online. They know I can see this, so are obliged to respond immediately.

As communication mediums have developed and continue to develop, it makes getting in touch with someone even easier. As online communication has become accessible to pretty much anyone it means more people are doing it and there is more competition as a jobseeker to be heard.

Jumping back to 1995, if I was looking for a job I would have purchased the local newspaper and scanned the jobs section. Finding something I was interested in applying for, I would have written a covering letter, popped it in an envelope along with a copy of my CV, written the destination address, attached a stamp and walked to the local post box to send it.

This all took effort and lots of it! How many jobs would I apply for and could I apply for? Not many is the answer, as the application process took time. As a result, I had to be very selective and targeted with my applications. Clearly, the more job adverts I responded to the better my chances and if I worked harder than other jobseekers I gave myself a far better chance of success. As the process took time and effort, it would put other jobseekers off applying.

Back then it was less likely that there would be a standard application form to complete, which meant that I could differentiate myself through the content and quality of my written communication. Ultimately, if I made the effort and put in the time I had a better chance of being heard, due to less competition and more scope to differentiate myself to an employer.

Nowadays it's too easy and takes no time at all to apply for a position or to send your CV – it's all done at the click of a button. With websites that provide a standardised platform for responding to advertised jobs, there is sometimes no longer a requirement to draft a covering letter – it's a box filling exercise and all applications received by an employer look the same, making it very hard for you to stand out. The move to standardised forms and processes has come about principally due to the volume of applications an employee will receive – they have had to put these filters in place.

I'll discuss more on how to stand out in the next chapter, and also in Chapter 9 where I'll explain my 'super secret advanced techniques'.

For now let's get back to the online 'You' and what I mean by this.

First of all, let's look at how employers and recruiters find candidates with the right skills for their business. Remember Conversation 3 from the last chapter? An employer who has exhausted his or her own network through Conversations 1 and 2 will either advertise a position on a job board or engage the services of a recruiter. But there is something else that an employer may do – can you guess what it is? It tends to be the bigger companies who have an internal resourcing team or a Human Resources function that will try this, often before they engage the services of a professional recruiter.

So what is it...?

Well... they sit down, switch on their computer and use the internet to directly find and then approach the person they are looking for! What this means is that if you the jobseeker do not have an online presence, no matter how relevant your skills are to an employer, they will never know about you as you can't be found.

Recruiters whose profession it is to find the best candidates in the market do this all the time as part of their job but employers are now sometimes doing this for themselves to avoid paying a recruitment fee and simply because they can – the internet is available to everyone and anyone.

There is now a double reason to be online – that's why the online 'You' is so important. But where to position yourself online and how?

Social media is defined on Wikipedia as *'the use of web-based and mobile based technologies to turn communication into interactive dialogue among organisations, communities, and individuals'*. As organisations are made up of individuals, it's really defined as technology used to facilitate communication between individuals or, better put for our purposes, communication between employer and jobseeker.

Talk to any teenager and they'll tell you all about social media; it's second nature to them, they use it every day to communicate with their friends, sometimes exclusively in place of face to face conversations. That's a very important point – in creating an online 'You' the purpose is not to avoid face to face conversations it's to create them.

Having an online presence is simply the start of a process with the ultimate aim of creating a face to face meeting.

It's rare that somebody hires a jobseeker they have never met and unless the world changes drastically in the future it's likely to stay that way. What has changed though is the way those face to face meetings are ultimately arrived at.

Let's get back to social media and the multitude of social networking platforms out there. The number will continue to increase, as social networking is big business and profitable business – just ask Mark Zuckerberg, the founder of Facebook. He floated his business and on the first day of trading made himself billions of dollars.

Some of the better known sites include:

- Facebook – **www.facebook.com**
- Twitter – **www.twitter.com**
- LinkedIn – **www.linkedin.com**
- Google+ – **www.plus.google.com**
- Pinterest – **www.pinterest.com**

In my business we use all of them, but each for different things. Some are seen as more personal than business, and since you, the jobseeker, are looking to engage with employers in a business relationship, we'll focus on the most important business platform here in my opinion, which is LinkedIn.

Before we go any further perhaps it's time for a word of warning. Although LinkedIn is going to be your primary tool in finding that next job, I imagine that many reading will have profiles on Facebook, Twitter and some of the other sites above.

It is important to be aware that if you are engaging with people online they will check you out online – trust me they will!

For example, Janet might have a highly professional, well constructed and composed LinkedIn profile, which she uses to contact a potential employer. The employer likes the look of her experience but decides to do some further research on Janet before inviting her in for interview.

They look up Janet on Facebook and because her privacy settings aren't set correctly they can see everything she got up to at the weekend and it's not a pretty site. Needless to say, the interview never happens and all goes quiet.

There's a lesson to be learnt here. Be aware of where else you have an online presence, even if it's for personal use, as business contacts may find you there too. Ensure your professionalism is consistent across the internet, wherever you might crop up, and bolt down your privacy settings on profiles you don't want to make public.

Ok, lecture over...let's get back to LinkedIn!

As a jobseeker, creating an online presence starts with creating an online profile on LinkedIn (**www.linkedin.com**).

The process is fairly easy – in simple terms, and as a bare minimum, your profile should be an online version of your CV.

A detailed explanation of how to create your profile on LinkedIn is outside the scope of this book for two reasons. Firstly there are better, more detailed books out there on this subject and secondly the platform is constantly evolving and developing, meaning that whatever I write will only stay up to date for so long.

To reassure you, when I first logged on to LinkedIn I had no real clue as to what I was doing. I knew I probably should be on there and simply followed the prompts which were fairly self-explanatory to create my profile. I was told that I needed to get 100% profile completeness and to do this I would need to complete all fields, make some connections and get recommended.

I now work a little bit on my profile everyday and as I've become familiar with the site it has got easier and easier to navigate and use – it's also been a very powerful tool in my business. My advice is to just get on there, create a profile and start using it. Nothing, in my experience, educates better than the experience of doing!

Your level of profile completeness sits visually as a bar on your profile home page, so it's really easy to see where you are and the platform is great at prompting you every time you log in to do something to increase this percentage. Your profile completeness is also a great indication as to whether something has changed on LinkedIn. If your profile completeness drops (mine has a couple of times) it means that there is probably some new additional work to do on your profile as a result of changes to the platform. You won't have to look far to find them, as LinkedIn will prompt you to get your percentage back up to where it was, or better! In the first instance, 100% profile completeness should be your primary target as you set up your profile – it's your first goal as a jobseeker new to LinkedIn.

For ideas on layout and content feel free to look at my profile (**http://uk.linkedin.com/in/simongraycherryprof**). I'm not claiming that I'm the number one expert or that my profile is perfect, but it might just help you in setting up yours.

Ok, so you've created your profile on LinkedIn – that's that then… the online 'You' is complete, right?

WRONG!

There's much more you need to do to get yourself seen.

Just to clarify – LinkedIn has a number of upgrades that you can make to your account, such as allowing you to email people you don't know via 'InMail', but this costs money. All of my tips in this chapter and throughout this book can be done with just a basic account. In fact, I have only ever used a basic account and now at the time of writing have over 1,300 connections. I'm not saying there isn't a place for the paid versions, but in my opinion, with a bit of thought and application the basic version offers massive opportunity and scope for doing what you need to do and best of all it's completely free!

So let's get back to building that profile.

Remember, as a jobseeker you need a LinkedIn profile so that employers interested in your skills and experience can contact you directly. But here's the distinction, and a massively important distinction at that! Being on LinkedIn doesn't guarantee that you will be seen or, better put, FOUND by a prospective employer. There are things you need to do having created your profile (which also help you achieve 100% profile completeness) that help people to find you.

Highlight 'Skills and Experience'

Remember I mentioned earlier that in simple terms your LinkedIn profile is an online version of your CV? Well to some extent it is and all I discussed in Chapter 3 on 'constructing a super CV' becomes relevant. That means don't just list your skills; make sure you quantify your achievements – what's the benefit to a prospective employer of contacting you?

Under 'Skills and Expertise' LinkedIn allows you to add skills from a searchable list that best describe your capabilities, so make sure you do. People viewing your profile can also endorse that you possess these skills.

Make 'Connections'

This point is very, very important and needs to be understood to maximise your visibility on the platform. There are three types of connections you can have on LinkedIn:

- 1st degree connections – people who are connected to you directly, e.g. my business partner Martin.

- 2nd degree connections – people your 1st degree connections are connected to, e.g. Martin's contact, John.

- 3rd degree connections – people your 2nd degree connections are connected to, e.g. John's contact Jenny.

In a nutshell, this means that the more people you connect to, the more people you can see and therefore, the more people you have in your network. By default, and more importantly, the more connections you have the more people and prospective employers that can see you.

The term 'connections' implies that you know the person well or that they're a trusted business contact. Indeed, before you go connecting to everyone and anyone, LinkedIn warns against adding complete strangers to your network, or accepting an invitation from someone you don't have a trusted relationship with. Given that it might be a potential employer that is looking to connect with you, each connection request should be judged on its own merits. Irrespective of who sends out the invitation, when it's accepted, both individuals are automatically added to each other's list of connections.

The easiest way to begin is to search for and connect with people you have worked with previously or know through your existing network. As you build your connections people will see you as a valuable contact and be keen to connect with you to expand their own personal network.

Join 'Groups'

LinkedIn allows you to join 'Groups' which are as described; groups of individuals on the site with a common interest, skill set or purpose. For example, as a member of the Institute of Directors, I am a member of the IoD's group on LinkedIn. Everyone else in this group is also member of the IoD, so it is a collection of like-minded individuals with a common interest and purpose. Some groups will be open, meaning anyone can join and others will be closed – for example, you can only join the IoD group if you are a paid up member of the IoD.

There is one overriding and primary reason for joining groups – it dramatically expands your network, i.e. the people you can see on LinkedIn. To be clear, it doesn't increase the number of your connections, but other members of the group are instantly visible to you in addition to the 1st, 2nd and 3rd tier connections discussed earlier.

Remember that the aim of the game is to be seen by potential employers – if you are in their network, by default they are in yours too. Also, remember that groups are about a common interest, skill set or purpose.

It's a bit like a single person looking to meet that someone special. They're likely to have a much better chance of meeting someone at an event organised for single people than they are popping down to the local pub, as the majority of the people in the room will be single and also looking to meet someone special – that's why they're there. The same is true online.

Get 'Recommendations'

If my LinkedIn profile says what a great recruiter I am, would you believe me? You might, but as I've made this claim myself it has less credibility than if someone else has said the same about me.

Just as an employer takes out references from previous employers on a candidate to get comfortable that their skills and experience are as described, using recommendations on LinkedIn enables you to give assurance about your abilities before any dialogue begins. Indeed, a great recommendation can be reason enough for a potential employer to get in touch with you about a new opportunity, so make sure you get some.

It's a fairly easy process – you connect with the person you're asking to make the recommendation, send them a request, then approve what they've written before it goes live on your profile. It's a good idea to give them a quick call before sending the request to check that it's ok – you're also likely to get it done quicker if they know it's coming and that it's important.

Here's an example of a recommendation taken from my LinkedIn profile:

"Simon has great enthusiasm for all tasks he undertakes and you can rely on him to come up with the goods. He is a great communicator showing good empathy with his clients. An eye for detail, firm views, decisive and with a sense of humour – these are all aptitudes I would associate with Simon."

Set 'Contact Preferences'

If you want employers to contact you about potential opportunities then you need to tell them. You can select your 'Contact Preferences' and at the very least need to tick that you are keen to be contacted about career opportunities. There is also a box where you are prompted to answer the question, *"What advice would you give users considering contacting you?"* In here I recommend you put both your phone number and email address.

Remember, your aim as a jobseeker is to get a face to face meeting and a phone call is far nearer to that than receiving an email.

'Contact Details'

It can be difficult for an employer to find your contact details in 'Contact Preferences', as it's hidden away at the bottom of your profile. It is always best to make things easy and obvious when you want someone to get in touch with you, so it's a good idea to put your contact details in a more obvious place. I recommend that you also put these details in your 'Professional Headline' right at the very top of your profile, as well as in the 'Summary' section – they have a much better chance of being seen!

Use 'Status Updates'

From the home page of your profile you are asked to answer the question, *"What's on your mind?"* This is a box where you can write anything you like, but sometimes it's best not to, particularly if you are having a bad day!

I'm not a fisherman, but there's an interesting parallel here with fishing which will help to illustrate why using this box to post regular status updates is important.

Imagine LinkedIn is a huge pond and the people in that pond are potential employers. Well, to catch fish a fisherman needs bait and bait is what you put in your status update to encourage employers to contact you ahead of anyone else.

Before we discuss what form this bait should take, as I'm not sure worms will do it, it's important to understand that every time you post an update it lands both on the home page of your profile and the home page of all of your connections – they can see what you are doing and what you are saying.

So back to the bait!

In my experience one of the worst things to do (remember the last chapter on networking) is to ask people outright for a job – there's no faster way to clear a room or lose interest from your online connections. On the flip side, one of the best things to do is to ask for help or advice. Human beings have a natural desire to help one another (hard to believe sometimes I know, but nevertheless it's true). We also like to give advice and have our opinions heard. Combine the two and you have a very powerful cocktail of communication.

As you know by now I'm a professional recruiter and also like real life examples, so here is one to illustrate this point.

A while back I was asked to recruit an IT Auditor by one of my clients. Now IT Auditors, as the saying goes, don't grow on trees or even bushes for that matter – they are very hard to find. My client – one of the biggest companies in the area, with its own internal resourcing team – had already told me that they had looked on LinkedIn for someone with suitable skills but without success.

At that time I had no IT Auditors on my database, so I was reliant on the internet, and principally LinkedIn, for a quick result – my clients don't like to wait too long! Undeterred by my client's failed attempt I went to LinkedIn and posted one status update, which took me less than a minute to write. This sourced me the right candidate, who I then met, presented to my client and who was ultimately offered the job – it can sometimes be that easy. From my experience on LinkedIn I knew that it was as much about how you write something as what you write. If I had just posted a link to a job advert with a message saying 'new vacancy', I'm pretty sure I wouldn't have got the result I eventually did! Instead I decided to ask my network to help me and to work for me to find the right person and posted a message that went something like this:

"Help or advice to find an IT Auditor for a Derby based client would be greatly appreciated – a fantastic opportunity for someone to join a great business. Please contact me at...or call..."

Within 30 minutes someone who used to work in the IT industry contacted me. I had never met or spoke to him before, yet he gave me the names of five people he recommended I contact through LinkedIn, which I duly did – one of whom got the job!

The other thing I did here was not only to post this as an update in my own profile; I also posted it as an update in IT Audit groups, which as expected reached a very targeted audience.

There are lessons to be learnt here:

- Asking for help and advice is a great way to start dialogue and generate results.

- Having a profile on LinkedIn is essential – if Neil (the candidate I placed) had not been on there I never would have found him.

Neil was actively looking for a new opportunity and had displayed his contact details clearly on his profile page, which made it easy for me to get in touch. Because I'd been recommended to contact him by someone he knew and trusted, I had a very warm opening for my first conversation. The power of the network is everything when used correctly.

Sticking with the IT sector for the moment let's look at another example of bait.

Instead of:

"Available immediately for IT work in the London area. Please call..."

Try:

"Looking to add value to an SME business with my IT skills, can anyone recommend people for me to contact please? Any help or

advice is much appreciated. I'm based in London and can be reached on..."

Now which is better? It should be obvious! What's also clever here is in the second update I am asking people to use their networks to help me. In the first update people are likely to ignore me unless they have a direct requirement for an IT specialist themselves. The distinction and difference here is very subtle but massively important.

I meet lots of jobseekers and always ask them if they are on LinkedIn and what their experience has been. The majority of people I meet now have a profile, and the number of professional people on LinkedIn has increased dramatically over recent years. When I ask most of the people I meet how they are using their LinkedIn presence proactively to find their next job, most look at me blankly, as if creating a profile was more than enough effort already! They are missing a trick. It's a bit like buying a car and never driving it – what's the point?

You have to make LinkedIn work for you and as an active jobseeker you should spend some time on the site each day – it needs to become a habit and part of your overall strategy to find that next position. At the very least you need to be doing the things discussed earlier in this chapter, but that's the bare bones.

As a quick reminder, you should be making connections, joining groups and asking for recommendations, in addition to regularly posting status updates.

What I've discussed so far draws a nice parallel with networking events discussed in the last chapter. It's a bit like turning up, standing in the corner and hoping someone comes over and talks to you! It's all a bit reactive and let's face it, it's what many people do at a networking event and even more so online. The difference is that at a networking event people know they should be proactive and approach other people they've never spoken to before, but online it's less obvious how this translates; the fact is that it does and there's so much more you can and should be doing.

So, building on the things you've learnt so far, let's take our LinkedIn profile to the next level; let's be proactive and let's get ahead of the competition. As I discussed in the last chapter, it's best to have a plan ahead of time as to who to engage with and how to do it. Online this is much easier; you don't have to think so much on your feet as you do at a networking event – you have more time to plan and prepare. So what should you be doing?

Commenting

Commenting constructively on people's status updates, and in particular on group posts in groups relevant to your industry or sector, is a great way to get noticed and to raise your profile. Providing your comments are professional, educated and add value, they will be well received and highlight you and your skills to a wider audience.

You shouldn't be asking for work or offering your services directly. If your comments are informative, an enquiry as to how you could help may naturally follow as the conversation progresses – remember nobody likes to be sold to!

If people have a problem on LinkedIn and you can solve it – then solve it! Give to receive and when the same individual or one of their connections has a bigger problem, they might just remember you and get in touch – you never know where things might lead.

Through careful and considered comment you can position yourself as an 'Industry Expert' – the go-to person when people need help. While it might not result in paid work initially, keep doing it and don't be surprised if you are invited to a meeting that results in a job offer.

Target marketmakers

Remember the power of the marketmaker from the last chapter? Well the same applies here.

Who in your industry and sector is active on LinkedIn? If they are active on LinkedIn, the chances are that they are well connected. Can you engage with them, arrange a coffee and build a relationship from there?

The answer is yes you can! It's the same approach as you took in the last chapter; it's just that the initial conversation happens online.

Target connections

You will know your industry far better than I. You'll know the businesses you'd like to work for and through LinkedIn can identify who's pulling the strings in those organisations. These individuals should be target connections and the people you want as your 1st tier connections.

LinkedIn can provide far more information on an individual than a company website and the information is more likely to be up to date. A company website is normally maintained by an IT department or an external web designer. Making changes and pushing through updates can often take time, which means you may be acting on out of date information and trying to contact someone in the business who is no longer there! This is not only a waste of time, it also tells the person who eventually reads your email or letter that you are out of touch with their business. Not very impressive really is it?

A great way to see if a company website is up to date is to look at their blog or news page. If the last article was written a few years ago, the chances are they don't bother updating things on a regular basis. On the other hand, if there are recent news items then you can take a punt that the other information on there is up to date and you can always check this with what's on LinkedIn to make sure.

LinkedIn has both 'People' and 'Company' pages and individuals with up-to-date profiles will probably be linked to their organisation's page. Where a company website is often faceless with little information about who is actually pulling the strings in the business, LinkedIn can not only give you a list of people within an organisation, it can tell you lots about them.

Advanced People Search (APS)

The APS allows you to search on 'Job Title' and 'Company' all within a given distance from a 'Postcode' that you can select. This means that you could search for Finance Directors within ten miles of your home or find the Operations Manager at ABC Ltd – it's that simple.

Once you have the name of the person you want to contact, you can utilise the skills I outline in the next chapter to 'get in front of the decision maker'.

Reading List by Amazon

What you read tells people lots about you. I explained in Chapter 3 that putting 'Reading' as a hobby or interest on your CV tells me nothing. What would tell me much more about you is knowing what you are reading. For example, if you are a web designer and are reading a book called *Latest Web Development Strategies*, it tells me that you have a real interest in your job and that your knowledge is bang up to date. It also provides some common ground for discussion, as if I've not read the book I'm probably keen to find out what's in it and if it's any good.

LinkedIn under the 'More' tab allows you to 'Get Applications', which includes the 'Reading List by Amazon'. You can find the book you are reading, comment on it and it sits on your LinkedIn profile for all to see.

People have yet another reason to contact you (if they have an interest in what you're reading) and you have a reason to contact others by expressing an interest in their reading material. It's not happened to me yet, but if someone contacted me through LinkedIn and asked for my thoughts on a book on my reading list I'd definitely get back to them. It's another great way of opening dialogue through a common interest.

Events

In the last chapter I discussed networking events and how to pick the right ones. LinkedIn has an application called 'Events' that allows you to search on events by topic and location. You can even click to say you will be attending and see who else is going before you arrive. This enables you to research the people you will meet and is a vehicle to better and more informative conversations on the day!

Search for Jobs

This is the most obvious way to use LinkedIn to find a job, but remember it's what your competition – namely other jobseekers – will also be doing.

Many businesses are now using LinkedIn to advertise jobs, in addition to using the more established job boards – it's another important reason for you being on LinkedIn. You can search for jobs by 'Job Title, Keywords, or Company Name' and the platform even tells you how many people have already applied!

Getting in front of the DECISION MAKER

Ever heard the phrase *"give to receive"*? Well, it really does work.

Think about it… if someone is offering you something for free that has value to you, aren't you more likely to engage with them than if they are hard selling you something you probably don't want or need?

When we started our business I took on sole responsibility for PR and marketing. My background is in accountancy and I have little experience in PR – still when you're at the start of something new on a limited budget it's amazing what you can turn your hand to! It helps that I have an interest in PR and marketing, as in my opinion it transcends all areas of life.

I had reasonable success and managed to get our brand out there in the market in local media, including magazines and through radio interviews. I was happy with my success and was definitely not looking for any help in this area – I certainly wasn't prepared to pay for any assistance! What happened next is a fantastic example of how to make an approach to someone you've never spoken to or had dealings with in the past.

I received an email from a guy called Greg. He complimented me on my success with PR and on establishing a brand presence in the market, as well as for winning a local business award for the 'most promising new business'. He communicated this in the first sentence of his email, which told me he had researched my business. This impressed me, as he'd taken the time to find out about my business and me and as a result I felt more inclined to read on.

I felt good about myself. Greg had complimented my efforts in PR. Now I'm no psychologist, but it's fairly obvious that people prefer to hear and are more receptive to positive comments – again I was curious and decided to read on. What Greg did next took me completely by surprise. He offered to write an article for me and to place it with one of the local business magazines – furthermore, he offered to do this for free!

So why would he do this? Greg was confident in his abilities and was prepared to demonstrate his skills in order to build a relationship. True to his word, he drafted the article (he did this from knowledge he had already built up on my business) and sent it to me for approval.

He suggested that we might meet up in the future over coffee, but didn't push this at all and nothing was put in the diary. I even told him that we weren't looking to bring anyone on board to do our PR as I was happy with the stuff I was doing – albeit it was taking me a bit of time each month.

When the magazine landed on my desk (and yes Greg did send me a copy) and I saw the published article, how do you think I felt? Well, I can tell you I felt great and was really pleased with the exposure but, more than that, I felt indebted to Greg. I was so grateful that I rang him straight away and thanked him for his help, we arranged a meeting at my office and the rest, as they say, is history.

Greg had shown me what he could do for my business by doing it. He hadn't sold to me, he'd simply shown me that he was an expert in his field and could add value over and above what I was doing already. Our meeting was therefore more of a chat, and at the end of it I signed him up on a monthly retainer to manage the PR for the business on an ongoing basis – that was two years ago!

Since then I've referred Greg to a number of my business contacts and two weeks ago he landed a big deal to provide PR services to one of my clients, a large manufacturing business with international operations – his biggest client win to date!

So, do you think the time Greg invested in writing that initial article was worthwhile? I'd say so!

But do you think we'd be working together if he'd sent me one of his brochures in the post and perhaps followed it up with a call?

Probably not – it's unlikely I'd have read the brochure, let alone take his call.

You see in business and also as a jobseeker looking for that next move, it's all in the approach or put another way – it's not what you say but how you say it!

"But how does this relate to me?" I hear you ask, *"I'm not a PR agent"* Well true, I accept you may not have magazine or radio contacts, but you have lots of other skills and experience to offer. Moreover, whether you think it or not, you are most definitely a PR agent. You are **P**ersonally **R**esponsible for promoting and marketing your abilities to a potential employer and for finding your next job. Other people can help you along the way, but the responsibility for you and your future success is totally down to you.

In the above example the approach could just as easily have been made by a jobseeker looking for an opening in my business. As I wasn't hiring at the time, a CV landing on my desk would probably have passed me by – but what if the same jobseeker had gone the extra mile like Greg? Perhaps they could have suggested I speak to a business contact of theirs who could potentially be a future client, or they could have sent me a document they had written on how to write a great CV. If they'd have done something different, they'd have been much more likely to get my attention and to get in front of me, as in their approach they would have demonstrated their skills and abilities.

Also, think about everyone else in the job market – what do they do? Well they do what they think should be done and don't think outside the box. They draft a covering email or letter, attach or enclose a CV and that's it as far as they're concerned – job done! They don't stand out from the crowd and then wonder why they don't get a result!

We discussed CV preparation in Chapter 3 and don't get me wrong, a CV is still an important and essential document. At some point during a recruitment process you are likely to be asked for it, but that doesn't mean it's the first thing an employer should see or needs to see from you – there are other things that you can and should be doing.

Now clearly I don't know your industry as well as you do. I won't understand the skills and abilities you have or how best these can be used to add value to a future employer, but the good news is that you will! Now, you might be reading this shaking your head but that's because you've never thought like I'm asking you to think before and that means it's difficult. Cast your mind back to first riding a bike – tough wasn't it? Now though it's easy; you don't even need to think about it.

Look at your industry and ask yourself:

- What's happening?
- What's important?
- Where can I add value?
- How can I best communicate this?

In Chapter 4 I talked about mapping your market and identifying the businesses and people you should be talking to – half the battle is already won! Now it's all about how to communicate with this target market to get noticed and to get a meeting to ultimately create your next opportunity. There are lots of mediums for communicating with and approaching a future employer, but to some extent the medium is less important – it's the message that counts. Having said that, this chapter would not be complete without discussing some of the mediums out there, along with the pros and cons of each.

Email

At the time of writing, this is the preferred and most over used form of communication. But what does that mean for you the jobseeker? It means that most people are using it in their job applications and as such it's much harder to stand out.

Think about the prospective employer. They're likely to receive hundreds of emails in their inbox every week on all topics and subjects, making it more likely that your email will be missed, lost or unopened. Worse still, your email might be seen as SPAM, end up in junk or be deleted outright. With so many emails flying about, and in an effort to keep on top of their inbox, an employer will delete without opening a high proportion of messages they receive and guess what… it's really easy to do – it takes one click of the mouse!

With any email, it's the subject line that has to stand out; this doesn't give you much space to communicate your message, which poses its own challenges. In some ways this is a good thing as you have to get to the point straightaway, but it can make life difficult.

Any attachment, no matter how good, is likely to remain unopened because it takes two clicks – one to open the email and one to open the attachment. Furthermore, with the ever present threat from viruses, people are less likely to open emails from people they don't know, and as such even less likely to open any attachment.

What this all means is that no matter how good your message it might just not get seen and your time and effort may be wasted.

Social media

I discussed 'the online You' and social media in the last chapter. As this is a newer form of communication than direct email, it's perhaps less understood and less abused, making it slightly easier to make yourself heard. The person you contact will also be alerted in their LinkedIn inbox in addition to their regular email inbox – they have two chances to see that you've been in touch, so you have a better chance of your message being read. Also, as your well written profile sits there for all to see, it's more likely that anyone you contact will click in to it out of curiosity to see who's been in touch and to find out what you're all about. Indeed, it's amazing on LinkedIn how often someone you look at looks back at you – try it and you'll see!

Note that when communicating using a medium like LinkedIn, you have limited characters. Any message you send has to be short and must get to the point quickly, which means you have to cut out any waffle – this is a good thing!

To connect with or message someone on LinkedIn you'll need to say how you know them. Options include 'Colleague', 'Classmate', 'We've done business together', 'Friend', 'Groups', 'Other' and 'I don't know'. Some will prompt you to enter an email address and if you've never met or had dealings with the person you're trying to contact, it can make life very difficult.

Contacting someone under the guise of 'We've done business together' allows you to send a message without an email address, but if you've never actually done business it's probably not the best thing to click. Think about the recipient of your message; they'll probably think you're trying to pull a fast one and it may not get you off to a good start! Be warned: contacting people in the wrong way, who then decline your connection can result in you receiving an email from LinkedIn like this:

Please note: *This message is a notice that you are nearing the threshold of "I don't know" responses you can receive before you will be required to enter an email address when sending invitations. Please remember to only invite people you know.*

Carry on and you could see your LinkedIn account suddenly disappear and then you'll have a whole load of hassle trying to get it back.

So how do you get in touch with people you don't know? Well the good news is that it's very easy, actually it's very, very easy indeed – that is once you understand the power of 'Groups'.

In the last chapter I advised that in creating your LinkedIn profile you should join groups. Not only does this quickly increase your network by making you more visible, it gives you a great reason to contact people you don't know.

Let's look at an example.

Tom Tucker (I've made the name up so please don't go looking for him) is someone I'm trying to reach on LinkedIn. I've found him through an APS, I have skills to offer his business and I want to get in touch. A quick glance at Tom's profile will tell me which groups he is in. Let's say he is in the 'Social Media Marketing' group – all I do is to join this group, wait until I'm accepted and then invite Tom to connect by selecting the 'Groups' option.

I write a quick personal message, which could go something like this:

"Hi Tom, we are both members of the Social Media Marketing group and I'm keen to connect on LinkedIn. I notice your business has just won a new contract, many congratulations. I'm keen to share some ideas with you if you'd like to get in touch. Best regards, Simon."

In a very short message I have done three things:

1. Demonstrated common ground with Tom by telling him we share the same group.

2. Taken an interest in his business by congratulating him on the new contract win.

3. Potentially sparked his interest with the phrase *"share some ideas"*.

A message like this is far more likely to generate a response from Tom and to open dialogue with him. There's no guarantee he will respond, but I've upped the probability considerably.

Letter

Communication by letter has been somewhat superseded in recent years by advances in technology.

Email is often preferred as delivery is instant – you press 'send' and your email shoots through cyberspace and lands in the recipient's inbox. It's also free (aside from the cost of your internet connection) and you don't need a stamp!

But a clear, well written letter still has its place and can be an extremely powerful tool and here's three reasons why:

1. Less people are writing letters which means that yours is likely to stand out.

2. A letter shows the recipient that you've made the effort – as it can be harder to write and is certainly more time consuming.

3. It's harder to ignore. If addressed properly, your letter is pretty certain to land on the recipient's desk and is likely to be opened by them in person. Again, curiosity kicks in and they have a burning desire to find out what's in the envelope.

Your letter and any enclosures might just sit around for a while, as it's harder to destroy. You can't just delete a letter without reading as you can with an email – it takes more than the click of the mouse. It probably involves a walk over to the shredding machine – many a letter I've received has been saved as I've read it on the way to the shredder! What this means is that letters are a great tool and something you should be using to approach your target audience.

Before I close on the subject of letters there are three tips I recommend for making sure your letter is opened, and more importantly opened by the person you've addressed it to:

1. Hand write the envelope – A typed envelope or typed sticker on an envelope or worse still a window envelope (with the address visible) says two things – mass mailer and impersonal. Hand writing your envelope in clear and legible writing gives you a much better chance of your letter being opened and read.

2. Mark your envelope 'Private & Confidential'. This means your letter is to be opened by the recipient only. While there is no guarantee a PA or secretary will not open it on the recipient's behalf, it significantly reduces the risk of this.

3. Always address the recipient in person. What I mean by this is don't address your letter to 'Dear Managing Director' or 'Dear HR Director' as this just shows lack of effort. A quick Google search, a look on LinkedIn or the company website, will highly likely give you the name of the person you're after.

If you still can't find the name of the person you're looking for, search in Google on their job title, company and news, e.g. 'managing director AND xyz ltd AND news'. It's often the Managing Director in a business who is asked to comment by the press on any business news; they are therefore often quoted and named in news articles.

Phone

The phone can be a great tool for getting to your target audience, but it can also be one of the most difficult mediums of communication. If it was as easy as picking up the phone and getting straight through to the person you want to speak to, then it really would be a great tool – providing of course that you'd prepared in advance what to say and how to say it.

The problem is that the person answering the phone (unless you have a direct dial number) is likely to be a gatekeeper whose job is to protect the person you're after from all unexpected and unwanted calls, including yours. Explaining to the gatekeeper why you are calling can be wasted effort and it also hampers your ability to call back, particularly if they've promised to pass on a message that may or may not get delivered.

My advice is that if you are using the phone to get in touch only discuss your offering with the person it is intended for – any other conversation is wasted time and can damage your chances of getting the conversation you want.

If you are struggling with a gatekeeper it's a great idea to call out of core business hours. The gatekeeper probably works standard hours but the person you are after probably doesn't and might still be in the business when you call early or late – it can be a great way to catch the person you want and to catch them by surprise. Try it, it's worked for me and it might just work for you!

Following up to get that meeting

Whatever the medium of your initial communication, the ultimate aim is to get a face to face meeting. Until you're face to face and having a conversation with the decision maker you're not quite there, so this always should be in the back of your mind as your primary goal.

A face to face meeting has moved you to the interview phase, which is the subject of the next chapter – this is where business really gets done and the chance of you being offered a job can, and often does, become a reality.

My advice is to use the above mediums not in isolation, but together. For example, a well placed letter with an interesting offering is sometimes just a well placed letter, until it's followed up with a phone call.

Let's face it, we're all busy. How often have you had something interesting come through the post that you put to one side to deal with later – it could be a special offer on a product you're really interested in that you would actually consider buying but what happens is that life gets in the way and you never get back to it.

A well placed and timely call after your letter lands could be well received. If the content of your letter is good it increases the chances of the person you're after taking the call. Using things in combination increases your chances of getting heard, being noticed and ultimately remembered.

Be careful though; don't email, phone, send a letter and post a message on LinkedIn all at the same time, as your target might feel they are being ambushed and be less inclined to respond. Spread things out, experiment and make sure you have fun with it – what's fun gets done and what's dull does not!

Remember, no two people are the same and what works as an approach to one person may not be the right approach for someone else. Some people like letters, some people are not good with email but prefer to talk on the phone, so do things in combination and at different times, as it gives you a far better chance of getting through in the most appropriate way. Your approach to a potential employer is essentially the same whether they are actively recruiting in the market or not or, put another way, whether they have a job or not.

I have lots of conversations with employers and always ask them if they have any jobs they are looking to fill at the moment. Often the answer is 'no' but when I probe a bit deeper and question, *"If I had someone with knowledge of your sector and also your IT systems what would you say?"* Nine times out of ten they're open to a face to face meeting, which might come to nothing but is still a face to face meeting!

In approaching companies directly, don't be disheartened just because you don't see a job advertised on their website – it's irrelevant. Remember, you're not approaching them and asking for a job; instead you are highlighting your skills and achievements in a different way. I can't tell you what the best way is as it depends on your industry. This is where you need to get creative and think back to Greg!

So who is the decision maker? In truth, it's sometimes hard to tell from the outside looking in.

Generally though, in businesses the people at the top of the organisation, for example the owner, Managing Director or similar, have the most decision making power and this should be the place you start. The good news is that they are often easier to find or to work out who they are, but the bad news is that they are often more difficult to get to.

One thing is certain and this is that information normally flows from the top down in an organisation and not the other way round – that's just the way things work. This means that it's always best to start at the top. If your skills and experience are of interest to the person at the top of the business, even if they are not the ultimate decision maker on bringing new people in, they will be able to point you in the right direction or refer you internally themselves, which is even better.

So far, we've talked about the direct approach to the decision maker in a business, but what if the decision maker has outsourced the decision and appointed a professional recruitment company to act for them?

Well it's a similar story. Getting noticed and taken seriously for a position by a recruitment company is extremely important. Think about it – recruiters handle multiple vacancies on a continued basis, many of which could be suitable for you. That's why it's so important to approach them in the right way, because they hold the keys to not just one door but many doors!

If you burn your bridges with a recruiter, no matter how relevant your skills are for a particular opportunity, you may still not make the shortlist. Professional recruiters are bombarded with emails and phone calls day in day out, so getting heard can be even more challenging. What differs in approaching a professional recruiter, as opposed to a business directly, is that a recruiter will always want a copy of your CV.

As discussed earlier, sometimes a CV is not the best thing to send to a decision maker in a business – remember Greg and how he thought outside the box? Nevertheless, a recruiter will always want a copy of your CV, as this is their product and what their clients will expect from them. They will also want this in an electronic format, even if your initial approach is not via email.

If you are approaching a recruiter about a specific job you've seen, then it's a great idea to call ahead of sending your CV and ask for a job profile so that you can best tailor your CV to suit. This approach helps a recruiter do their job, as their clients are looking for candidates who at first on paper match the job specification they've produced – your efforts will be welcomed!

A good recruiter will normally hold a generic copy of your CV on file but ask you to tailor your CV to specific job roles as and when they arise. Offering to make this additional effort in your first communication tells them that you are serious and committed. In my experience, candidates that are serious and committed are treated more seriously by and worked harder for by recruiters.

Remember, your aim is always to get in front of a decision maker and that includes recruitment consultants, as they decide whether your CV goes forward for not just one job but multiple jobs. If you offer to meet a recruiter in office hours you'll get a better response than if you suggest an evening meet – we have families and lives to get home to too! Although the meeting is with a recruiter and not a direct employer, you must treat it like a job interview. I'll cover this in more detail in the next chapter.

Tips for dealing with recruiters – what to do and what not to do

Lose the chip on your shoulder

You may have been out of work for a while and are feeling down on your luck or you may have had a bad experience with another recruitment company in the past – whatever you do leave both at the door!

I recently interviewed a candidate who told me that he'd had bad experiences with other recruitment businesses, he'd expected them to find him a job and they hadn't – as such he wanted to see if my business was any different! How positive do you think I felt about that candidate and how well do you think that meeting started?

I probably don't need to answer that one.

I knew instantly why this guy had a bad experience with recruiters and why they had not put him forward to interview – it's because he had no respect for them! They would no doubt be nervous (as I was too) that he would carry this chip on his shoulder in to interviews with their clients and damage relationships with businesses that we as recruiters work so hard to build.

Ask for help

As discussed earlier in this book, asking for help is a great idea. As human beings we are naturally programmed to help one another and, when asked, most likely will.

When a jobseeker asks for my help they are saying two really positive things to me:

1. I value your opinion and professional expertise.

2. I will listen to what you tell me and do what you ask me to do.

I am very likely to go out of my way to help a jobseeker like this because I know my efforts will be rewarded. Because they respect my abilities and will act upon my advice they make themself a better candidate, which makes it far easier for me to help them find a job.

Don't tell them how to do their job

Nothing is more annoying than being told how to do your job in whatever profession and the same is true in recruitment.

A brain surgeon probably doesn't have this problem as very few people have any knowledge at all about brain surgery. The problem in recruitment is that anyone who has recruited or moved jobs automatically thinks they know how to do recruitment, but nothing could be further from the truth. It's a bit like someone assuming they know how a car works just because they drive one – it's not that simple.

If recruitment were simple then everyone would be doing it. It's not and can be an extremely complicated process that intertwines skills, experience, motivations, emotions and lots more than that. As a jobseeker, give the recruiter what they need and then leave them to get on and do what they do best. Take on board advice and implement that advice and you're well on your way to building an excellent and fruitful relationship with your recruitment consultant that will last for years.

Don't tell them why you are right for a job – show them

Lots of the jobseekers I interview tell me they're right for a job because they are very commercial and great with people. Sounds good doesn't it, but what does it mean? Not much really, as anyone can say these things.

A recruiter needs to convince their client to invite you in for interview – saying to their client that they should see you because you are commercial and good in person just won't wash. They'd have to have a fantastic relationship with their client to get you an interview on that information alone.

Remember my explanation of the importance of achievements – well are you **READY?**

REA – **REA**lity.

DY – **D**id **Y**ou do?

? – Well, so what?

It's far better to give a recruiter a clear and concise example of where you've added value in the past – it gives them the tools or ammunition to get you that interview. Have your achievements at the forefront of your mind – they are factual, they have substance and most of all they're impressive! Help your recruitment consultant to help you and they'll go all out to help you find that next job!

Keep in touch

When I meet jobseekers and ask them about their experience with other recruitment businesses they often tell me that they registered a few months ago but haven't heard anything since. They are peeved that the recruiter has not been in touch and also that they are still on the job market.

At the start of this chapter I talked about PR in the context of Public Relations, but also Personal Responsibility. Remember, the responsibility for finding your next job lies with you and you alone – yes, that's you the jobseeker and nobody else! Recruiters can help you on this journey, but there are no guarantees.

In its simplest form, a recruiter talks to clients to generate jobs and sources candidates to fill those jobs – that's how they get paid and that's how they put food on the table. Generally there are more candidates than jobs, so if a recruiter were to keep in touch with every jobseeker they've met on a weekly basis they'd have no time to call clients and generate the jobs to place their candidates in.

Which would you rather – a recruiter who calls you week in week out but never finds the job you're looking for or one that calls you less regularly but when they do it's usually about a job? If I was on the job market I know which I'd prefer.

There is nothing to stop you the jobseeker keeping in touch with your recruiter via email or phone every couple of weeks though. This has advantages as it:

- Keeps you in the forefront of their minds.

- Keeps them up to date with your job search and shows you are still active and looking for that next move.

Weekly is too often and can be annoying. Furthermore, calling on the same day and at the same time can become predictable and even more annoying. Mix it up a bit and try and always call with something to say. Have you had feedback on an interview elsewhere that they need to know about or have you seen an opportunity on the website that you're interested in?

Help your recruiter

Why is it that sometimes when I call a client they don't call me back, but when I call them as a candidate they call me back instantaneously? Funny isn't it – the same person but a totally different reaction depending on my approach.

In my business above a certain level candidates and clients are one and the same. We are often recruiting for someone who is also active in the job market – we represent them on both sides of the fence.

I talked earlier about giving to receive and it really does work a treat. A professional recruiter, whether they tell you or not, will be keen to understand the organisational structure of your current business, or last business if you are out of work. You moving jobs will potentially create an opportunity for another jobseeker and this domino effect is an important factor in keeping the job market moving.

Volunteering information on your current business and also other businesses that you've worked for to your recruiter will really cement you in their thoughts and they'll be massively keen to return the favour and help you find that next move.

Life, in my opinion, really is all about relationships and the relationship between recruiter and jobseeker is just another business relationship that runs both ways. The problem is that jobseekers often don't see it like this. Appreciate this early on in your conversations with recruiters and you really will help yourself and encourage them to help you.

I'm conscious that I've preached about the way to deal with and approach recruitment businesses. I've not done this out of ego, but out of necessity, as so many jobseekers do it so badly.

A good relationship with a great recruiter really has power over and above what you can do off your own back in three areas and these are worthy of a brief explanation below:

1. A recruiter can talk directly to an employer about you. There is less reliance on a piece of paper, usually the CV, as a good recruiter brings this to life and highlights your key skills and achievements and also gives the employer their thoughts on your personality, which is harder to glean from a piece of paper. A good recruiter will have an opinion and will provide a recommendation to their client that they should meet you.

2. A good recruiter is a good sales person and often will sell your skills and experience to a potential employer better than you can do yourself. Not everyone is good at selling; don't get me wrong, we all need to do it, but recruiters are experts and do it very well indeed – they might open a door for you that you may have otherwise found shut.

3. You are not alone! A good recruiter may have extensive experience of recruiting for the same business. They are likely to know the type of interview you'll face, the personalities of the interviewers and, more importantly, what they will be looking for. Your recruitment consultant can prepare you properly for interview and guide you in your interview preparation, which I discuss in the next chapter.

Delivering a
FIRST
CLASS
INTERVIEW

So, you've planned out your job search, written a fantastic CV and been in touch with decision makers and now you've been invited in for a meeting. A meeting with a potential employer, however described, is an interview and there is a big distinction. An interview is something that strikes fear into the hearts of many and most people dread. Badge something as an interview and many jobseekers go weak at the knees, break out in hot sweats and lose the ability to speak. Despite having worked hard to get in front of the decision maker and now having a golden opportunity all is undone by a combination of nerves and poor interview technique.

In this chapter I'll cover both areas and by the end you'll have all the tools you need to deliver a first class interview, giving you the best chance of being offered a job!

So let's get back to that word 'interview'. Personally I don't like it, and for two good reasons you shouldn't like it either. Firstly, as described already, it sends people in to a panic! Secondly, it implies one way traffic – i.e. the potential employer has the power, asks the questions and makes the decisions.

In my opinion, any interview with a potential employer is simply a meeting. Yes, that's it – a meeting of two individuals who are looking to identify common ground and to establish whether they can work together.

Having the right mindset as a jobseeker is massively important for any meeting with a potential employer. From now on then, and for the remainder of this chapter and book, I will refer to 'interview' as 'meeting' because plain and simple that's what it is.

Let's look at some facts:

1. Although you may have initiated the approach using the techniques outlined in this book, the employer has agreed to, or better still requested, the meeting. You haven't begged or put a gun to their head to persuade them!

2. As human beings we meet people every day, so why should a meeting with a potential employer be any different or any more nerve racking?

3. No matter who you are meeting, they breathe the same air, they get up in the morning and go to bed at night and yes, they still have the bodily functions we all do and use the toilet! They're nothing special and are not to be feared, no matter how successful they've been or how rich they are!

This may sound strange and it's possibly not what you expected to find at the start of this chapter, but having the right mindset and attitude prior to interview is so important. This doesn't mean as a jobseeker you should be complacent or cocky – it definitely doesn't mean either of these. What it does mean is that you should be confident and prepared! Confidence in part comes from the right mindset but also from preparation, which will be a major focus of this chapter.

I've talked a little about mindset and it's now time to get in to the detail of how to best prepare for your meeting with a potential employer. I appreciate that changing your mindset overnight can be difficult, but following the advice on how to prepare will naturally empower you and build your confidence ahead of the meeting.

In my line of work I'm often asked to speak on the radio and comment on the latest unemployment figures or anything else job related. The researcher from the radio station normally calls me and sets up a time for me to speak to the presenter live on air, usually later that day. Sometimes I have read something about the topic to be discussed in the newspaper and sometimes I haven't, but I have an opportunity. The window between the researcher's call and going live on air gives me an opportunity to prepare!

If I'm interviewed cold, despite having been on the radio many times, I know there's a chance I'll clam up, get hot under the collar or not be able to think straight, so I use the time ahead of the interview to research the story, decide where I stand on the subject and what my opinion will be and know which points I want to get across to the radio presenter. By the time I'm live on air, I'm calm, confident and have a clear and concise message to communicate.

You have the opportunity to do exactly the same ahead of any meeting with a prospective employer and I'll now show you how.

When I ask most jobseekers how they prepare for an interview they give me a standard answer. They tell me they look at the company's website. When I push them further and ask what else they've done they often look confused and surprised.

Think about what you're trying to do as a jobseeker – remember you're trying to stand out and get ahead of the competition. What do you think everyone else does ahead of his or her meetings? Well I can tell you, they do the same as you and that's look at the company website – nothing more, nothing less! Looking at the company's website is the absolute bare minimum, but there is so much more you can and should be doing to stand out. Researching the business is also only half the story. What about researching and knowing yourself?

This is perhaps best illustrated by a real-life example.

A number of years ago I sent a candidate for interview with one of my big clients – let's call her Barbara. I was confident sending Barbara as she had all the right experience for the position and had researched the company well – but despite all this she failed to get the job. I asked my client for feedback and they explained that when asked about a specific skill set Barbara had failed to come up with an example. Don't get me wrong, we all struggle at times to come up with relevant examples, so I probed a little further. My client was really frustrated as Barbara had on her CV as an achievement a brilliant example of the skill set they were asking about – in fact that's why they'd asked the question! Clearly Barbara had not read her CV or researched herself, which proved to be her downfall – she never made the same mistake again.

So let's look at these areas in turn and understand how to research the prospective employer you are meeting and also how to research yourself. I'll then put it all together and run through the mechanics of the meeting.

So let's begin!

How to research the employer

Any employer comprises two things – the company and the person you're meeting. What this means is that it's just as important to research the person you're meeting as well as their company or business. Doing this research is so important because it shows the employer that you are seriously interested in their business. It also makes for a more productive meeting as you have a platform of knowledge at the outset – more on this in the mechanics of the meeting.

Let's look at both areas:

Researching the company

1. Company information – in the UK you can find out information on finance and ownership at Companies House – **www.companieshouse.gov.uk** (there will be similar organisations in other countries). For a nominal fee you can download the latest accounts and other company information.

2. Website – I've mentioned the website earlier and highlighted that as a bare minimum this is what everyone does ahead of any meeting. But there is looking at a website and looking at a website. Most people will have a quick glance at the 'About Us' page and that's about it but there's far more too it than that. Take a look at the 'Products' and 'News' pages in particular. The 'News' page normally contains a wealth of information about what the business is currently doing or planning to do. It's badged as news on their website as they're proud of it, keen to promote it and, more importantly, will be more than happy to talk about it.

3. Experience the business – think about the business you are meeting with. Do they have outlets or a product that you can experience? You might be meeting the owner of a retail organisation. How powerful would it be to visit one or more of the shops, chat to the manager on site about what's

happening in the business and perhaps even get an insight in to the person you will be meeting? Thinking outside of the box like this really sets you apart from the competition. The fact that you've made the effort is often more important than any information gained. It tells the person you are meeting a lot about your interest in his or her organisation. There might not be a shop front but there can be other ways to experience any business – it just requires some thinking.

For many years I recruited for a regional airline and encouraged my candidates to experience the product. Now the ideal way to do this would be to take a flight but given the cost consideration and lead time to interview this was not always possible. Instead, what was possible – and also more cost effective – was to get online and experience the flight booking process first hand (the booking could easily be aborted prior to checkout). Was it easy, what other information could it provide and what feedback could you give the person you're meeting?

4. Company literature – what does the company you are meeting with send out to their customers and more importantly have you read it? Phoning up reception or an organisation's marketing department and asking them to post out some publicity material is a great idea. They may refer you to the website as a source of information, but be firm and request hard copy information in the post. It's important and has another use, which I'll explain shortly.

5. Internet search – a Google search on the business can throw up lots of information that you won't find on the website. It's really important you do this on the morning of your meeting to identify any latest news that may or may not have made it on to the company's website as yet. Imagine that the business I'm meeting has won an important contract on the day of my meeting. Do you think I should know about it and, more importantly, don't you think the employer would expect me to know about it?

6. Market information – do you think knowing something about the industry that the business your meeting operates in would help? Well, absolutely yes it would. There is lots of free information on the internet that gives a flavour for a particular market sector on what's happening and what's important. Key Note (**www.keynote.co.uk**) is one such website and there are many others. Key Note offers paid industry reports but also offers a free Executive Summary. I particularly like Key Note's strap line – 'Transforming knowledge in to success' – so true! Having market information on the industry in your arsenal is of great value and will help in framing great questions, which I'll cover later in this chapter.

Researching the individual

Get online – in Chapter 6 I talked about the online 'You' and specifically LinkedIn. Make sure you have looked at the person you're meeting's profile. What's their background and where have they worked in the past? Where were they educated and did you attend the same school or university? What do they do outside of work and what are their hobbies and interests? Also, what are they posting in their status updates? What does this tell you about their current thinking and what's important in their business? Do you have any contacts in common – who do you know that they know? LinkedIn is a great tool to find this out as you can easily identify any 2nd tier connections you have in common.

At this stage it's best not to connect directly with the person you are meeting. It's a bit early to be doing this, but there's nothing to stop you viewing and researching their profile. How powerful to be able to talk to someone who knows the person you're meeting ahead of time, to gain an insight into their personality and also what makes them tick!

Do you remember the three conversations from Chapter 5?

A contact in common who you both know and trust, even though they are not present at the meeting, gives both sides credibility and confidence. It can also put you ahead of the competition who may not have a common relationship, or worse still may not have identified it and therefore not leveraged it!

How to research yourself

Know your CV inside out – knowing yourself and your experience by putting together a great CV is a fantastic starting point in researching yourself. I discussed this in Chapter 3 so won't labour the point here, apart from to say that once you've written it, make sure you read it ahead of every meeting to remind yourself what's on it. As my earlier example of Barbara illustrated, it can be easy to forget!

Focus on what's important – prior to any meeting there are things you can do to identify what's specifically relevant about your experience to the person you're meeting and their business. Communicating all of your skills and experience at a meeting is not only very boring it's also impossible. This means you have to identify and communicate what's most relevant to give yourself the best chance of being offered the job.

A quick question – when's best to identify what's most relevant? Before or during the meeting? Well, if you're thinking too much at a meeting then you're probably not listening and that can be dangerous, so beforehand is always best!

If a job specification has been produced then it's a good idea to obtain this in advance. Take a piece of A4 paper and draw a line down the middle. Next, read the job specification three times then put it face down. On the left hand side of the paper write down the four or five key things that are important in the role. Next, read your CV through three times and again place it face down. Now, in the right hand column write down opposite the four or five key things important in the role, examples of your experience and, more essentially, achievements in these areas.

Remember point six above on market information? Now that you know what's happening in the sector, what does that tell you about the skills and experience a potential employer might need? I can't give you the answer as you know your skills and experience along with the sector you operate in far better than I do. What I'm certain of though is that there will be certain trends in your industry that will make certain skills and experiences more important than others – these are the ones you should focus on!

Putting it all together – the mechanics of the meeting

Ok, so you've done the research and now know lots about the person you're meeting and their business – now let's get in to the mechanics.

Where you meet is not particularly relevant but getting there on time most definitely is. There is only one way to be on time for a meeting and that's to be early. Now let me be clear, when I say early, I'm talking five or ten minutes at the most not half an hour! The person you're meeting is likely to be busy running his or her business and may find it irritating to find you in reception too early. You need that five or ten minutes to sign in, pick up your name badge and for the receptionist to call to let the person you are meeting know you've arrived. Even if you arrive bang on time, you could be perceived as being late due to the time it takes to check in!

There are two major obstacles that get in the way and can make you late – recognise them beforehand and deal with them as follows:

1. Getting lost – the best way to avoid this is to do a practice run a few days before. This enables you to pinpoint and know exactly where you need to be.

2. Traffic – you can't determine the traffic or predict an accident but you can prepare for both. Leave early and allow plenty of time to get to your destination and make sure you've added a bit more time on just in case. On the test drive it's a good idea to identify a nearby café. If you arrive with plenty of time to spare, take the opportunity for a quick coffee round the corner to ensure you arrive at your destination only five to ten minutes early.

The last thing you want to do is arrive in a last minute panic, hot, stressed and flustered. Remember, your mindset is important, so plan ahead and make sure you arrive calm and composed.

Before I leave this section, let's talk a little bit about dress code or what you should wear to create the best impression.

As discussed already – it's important to fit in and mirror certain expectations in your industry, as well as doing your best to stand out and be remembered. One such expectation is how you present yourself and the clothes you wear. This will differ from industry to industry. A male banker in the City will be expected to wear a shirt, tie and smart suit, whereas a graphic designer might be better received with no tie and in more casual attire.

It can be hard to get this right and as a rule of thumb, or if in doubt, a shirt, tie and business suit for men and a jacket and skirt or trouser suit for women rarely offend. Also, don't forget the little details, as they are just as important. For example, is your shirt or blouse ironed and are your shoes polished?

Investing in your appearance, whether it's a haircut or a new pair of shoes, can be a double whammy. It shows the employer that you take pride in yourself, have attention to detail and are likely to bring both qualities to his or her business. In addition, looking good means feeling good and also confident. Having a confident mindset for a meeting with a potential employer, as I discussed earlier, is very important.

Now you've arrived when does your meeting start?

Sounds like a silly question doesn't it? Well it's not, and so many jobseekers fall at the first hurdle because they think the meeting starts when it starts or, better put, when you come face to face with the person you are meeting… but it doesn't.

Let me tell you what I do in my business.

After I've met with someone and am in the process of deciding whether they are right for our business, I consult with everyone who has come into contact with them. I ask the receptionist at the office what they thought and how they communicated and ask anyone in the office who has spoken to him or her on the phone for their opinion.

You see, people often come across differently to different people and an interview or meeting is a somewhat artificial environment where a jobseeker arrives with their game face on. But what are people like when their guard is down and they think they are away from the watchful eye of the person they are trying to impress?

You are in the meeting as soon as your car comes within sight of the employer's premises and remain in the meeting until you leave and are out of sight again.

Think about this. What if you pass the time with the receptionist and he or she tells the person you're meeting after you've left how friendly and polite you were. Could this help your cause? What if you leave the business premises and immediately whip your tie off, jump in your car and speed out of the car park. Does this create a good impression? Just two examples, but clearly the first gives a positive impression and the second a different impression altogether.

Ok, so you're standing in reception – yes, that's standing not sitting down. But why is this important? Surely it doesn't matter or make a difference if you sit down, does it? Actually it does, and it's all down to the psychology of the meeting and who has control. I touched on this earlier and getting it right really sets the tone for the whole meeting and what happens afterwards.

Get this right and you set yourself miles apart your competition – so far apart in fact, that there is only one decision to be made, which is that you get hired!

The mindset for your meeting should be that it's a meeting of minds. It is definitely not poor desperate jobseeker meets powerful employer who possesses all the power and will make that make or break decision – approach a meeting like this and you set yourself up to fail. You are equals and the potential employer has as much to gain from hiring you as you do from being employed – it's that simple.

Take this a stage further and think about who controls an interview (I've switched back to this term temporarily for ease of explanation). Sounds a silly question, doesn't it? Surely it's the employer or interviewer who controls the interview, as they're the one asking the questions. In normal circumstances it is the employer, but what I'll show you shortly is how you, the jobseeker, can control every aspect of the meeting to your advantage and the employer will never even notice. Indeed, the employer will find the interview process extremely easy and productive and may credit this to his or her extraordinary interview skills, when really it was all down to you.

Part of any recruitment decision boils down to how well a prospective employer gels with a jobseeker; the smoother the meeting goes, the more chance the employer walks away and thinks, *"Well that went well!"* This can only be good news for you and your quest to find employment – at the very least it's not bad news is it?

But before I get to this – why is it important as a jobseeker to control the interview? The overriding reason is that so many employers are absolutely terrible at interviewing. They are bad at it for two reasons:

1.   They don't do it very often, so have little practice.

2.   They don't enjoy it as it is outside of their comfort zone.

The exception tends to be in bigger companies where an experienced Human Resources professional takes charge and runs the process. In smaller businesses that recruit less often, the responsibility usually falls to the owner or manager, who is likely to have little experience and therefore little confidence in this area.

So let's get back to reception and run through my top tips to control the meeting process from the outset. Remember you were back there STANDING up in reception:

Standing room only – Stand up in reception don't sit. Standing up puts you on the same level as the employer from the outset psychologically. You both start from the same position and it reduces any awkwardness in trying to get out of that comfy armchair that you've sunk into. As you're already standing it's also harder to relax. You want to be calm ahead of the meeting, but not relaxed. Stood up, alert and ready you are better prepared to make a great first impression.

Breaking the ice – You now move in to the second phase of control. Gemma (we'll bring the employer to life now) greets you in reception. Start with a firm handshake while you look her in the eye – don't stare, but look her in the eye confidently. This is no time to be offering a wet fish so make sure your handshake is firm, but by the same token it's not a test of strength – if you hear knuckles crunching, you've gone too far. As with anything, practice makes perfect, so practice your handshake ahead of time and get it right. This is a great time to break the ice and let Gemma know you've done your research. This is in the form of a well placed question or comment along the lines of:

"I noticed the picture on the wall in reception, is that of your facility in China?"

"I understand you've just won a new contract today, many congratulations. I imagine that's been very positively received across the business hasn't it?"

Don't worry if Gemma hasn't heard the news on the new contract win – if she hasn't, great, it gives you the opportunity to tell her about it!

Also, remember the publicity material you sourced in advance of the meeting from the marketing department and have read cover to cover? How convenient as it's tucked under your arm for Gemma to see – now's a great time to tell her that you've read it!

Your initial icebreaker could be more personal, for example:

"I hear that you're a keen tennis player, have you been watching Wimbledon?"

The last thing you want as you walk to the meeting room is a stone cold silence and discussing the weather is just a wasted opportunity. Take control of the icebreaker and take control of the interview.

To drink or not to drink? I have two thoughts on this and it depends in part on you the jobseeker. If you are a clumsy person and likely to knock a drink over, then don't have one - getting out a mop and bucket is no way to start a productive meeting - trust me, I've done it! On the other hand, there is a school of thought that says sharing a drink (a hot drink apparently works best) helps to build rapport. Furthermore offering to help make the drink or chatting to Gemma while she makes it further breaks the ice before you get down to business.

Be first - In my spare time I box; it's a great stress buster and is a good balance to working in an office. We have a saying in my boxing club, which is *"be first"*, and although in a meeting while it's unwise to come to blows, the principle holds true. In boxing, if you strike your opponent first you put them on the back foot and have a better chance of controlling the fight - the same is true in a meeting. Let's look at two ways the meeting might start:

Gemma - *"Thanks for coming across today, I thought I'd start by giving you a run through what we do at ABC Ltd."*

You - *"Gemma, thanks so much for meeting up with me today. Just to let you know before we start that I've done a fair bit of research on your business, including visiting one of your stores and reading your company brochure."*

Which sets the scene for a better interview?

Which keeps you in control?

Which is more impressive?

If you think the second option answers all of the above, you'd be right. Gemma now knows you have a high level of base knowledge on her business, so she can engage with you at a higher level. She's impressed that you've taken the trouble to research and have done more than other people she has met. You've 'hit first' and taken control.

Ask questions - It's very easy to get stuck in a rut at a meeting, with Gemma firing questions and you sitting there responding. It gets boring and makes it very difficult to build rapport. Rather than engaging dialogue, the meeting turns into one-way traffic of question, followed by answer, followed by question and so on and so on.

In any meeting there's always a series of questions and answers, but it doesn't mean the same person should always be asking the questions with the other person answering – it shouldn't work that way and doesn't have to.

For example:

Gemma – *"As you know, we're in the process of expanding our operations overseas. Can you talk me through the skills you have in this area which are most relevant please?"*

Now clearly you need to answer the question, if you don't you'll look pretty silly. But how about finishing your answer with:

You – *"...what do you think are the most important skills to possess to give the biggest contribution in this area?"*

Or:

You – *"...which skills have you developed as a result of your involvement with the international expansion?"*

The latter response is more inquisitive and higher level and as such, you might not be comfortable including such a response in your arsenal. If this is the case, that's absolutely fine – stick to something you feel more comfortable saying, but think outside of the box and try out this strategy as it works extremely well!

Are you READY? – Remember in Chapter 3 where I showed you how to construct a clear and concise achievement? Whether you are responding to questions or volunteering information, use this technique to communicate effectively. It works just as well for verbal communication as it does for written.

Clothe the robot – Despite the automated world we live in, no one employs a robot. Sure, you are using techniques and strategies to deliver the performance of your life, but don't let on to the employer. Just as a good actor is natural, believable and easy to watch, you must be too. So make sure you clothe the robot and hide the machinery underneath!

Fill in any blanks – Remember, Gemma may not be the best at asking questions that give you the best opportunity to highlight your relevant skills and achievements. But remember who's in control – it's your responsibility to get this information across.

Imagine you know from your research that ABC Ltd is looking at changing its IT system. Gemma has asked you nothing about this, but you've had experience of driving two successful system implementations in the past. Don't you think Gemma should know about your previous experience? If this happens, you need to be ready and towards the end of the meeting you might say:

"Gemma, just before we finish, I know from the research I've done on your business that you're looking to implement a new IT system within the next 12 months. I've driven two successful system implementations in the past but am conscious we've not covered this?"

Notice here that you're not forcing this information on Gemma, you're just directing her to ask a question about your experience in this area. She may have forgotten to ask it and you've just given her a subtle prompt or she may have evidenced all she needs in this area from your CV. Who cares what the reason is – you're in control and it's your responsibility to bring this up – it also shows once again that you've done extensive research on her business.

One word of caution – make sure you adopt this tactic towards the end of the meeting. You don't want to jump the gun and she may have been planning to ask about this a bit later. As with anything, timing is important and in the heat of battle you'll naturally get a feel for when the time is right.

Ask killer questions – The first rule of asking great questions is never ever ask anything you could find the answer to yourself. It's just plain lazy and is a wasted opportunity. Instead, ask things that build on your existing knowledge – or put another way, ask knowledge-based questions:

"Gemma, ahead of our meeting today I read a Key Note report on the industry which suggested that increased demand for your products is

likely to come from abroad over the next few years. Is this something you're finding as yet?"

Boom! A killer question just hit home. Clearly and concisely you've told Gemma that you've researched extensively, have some knowledge and want to know more.

Contrast this with, *"Gemma, which countries do you sell your products to?"* Didn't you look at the website?! Make sure that your questions display your knowledge, not your lack of it.

Never ever ask about salary or other benefits. These are not knowledge-based questions. Instead, rest assured that the more you impress at interview, the better positioned you are to negotiate the best remuneration package possible! If Gemma asks what you are looking for tell her what you are currently on (or if you are out of work what you earned in your last role), but emphasise that the opportunity is more important and this is an opportunity you are extremely interested in!

Say what you thought – at the end of the meeting both parties often walk away not knowing what the other person thought. But why? Wouldn't it save time and be helpful to know?

If you enjoyed the meeting then now's the time to tell Gemma:

"Gemma, thank you for your time today, I've really enjoyed our meeting and am extremely keen to further explore opportunities/potential opportunities with your business. Given what you've heard today do you have any further questions for me or any reservations about my suitability that I may be able to clear up now?"

Having made the first move and remained in control you might just leave the meeting with an idea of what she thinks!

Create a reason to get in touch – Is there a reason for you to contact Gemma after the meeting? Did she mention something that you can help her with or do you have any information she could find useful? The Key Note report you asked about, maybe Gemma hasn't seen it and you could send it to her?

Keeping the dialogue going is a great idea, as the more regularly you can communicate the quicker you will build rapport. Look for opportunities in the meeting to keep in touch and bring them up at the end.

If you've ever travelled first class, stayed in a five star hotel or experienced outstanding customer service in a restaurant, how do you feel? You feel great don't you? More to the point, you'll remember the experience and probably can't stop talking about it!

It's your responsibility using the techniques outlined in this chapter to not only deliver but control what turns out to be a first class experience for the employer. It takes some practice but you now have the skills to stand out from the crowd, be remembered and get offered the job you want!

SUPER SECRET

SECRET

advanced techniques

n the preceding chapters I've given you the skills to empower your job search and to be successful in the increasingly competitive job market.

I've purposefully held some things back that if I'd mentioned too early might have seen you running for the hills screaming, *"There's no way I can do that!"*

Remember, by getting to this stage of my book and through implementing the techniques and strategies outlined so far, you are already light years ahead of the average jobseeker. Remember him or her? Sat at home browsing jobs on the internet, waiting for something to happen? You've now turned this on its head and rather than waiting for the market to come to you, you are out there attacking proactively with new vigour and confidence.

While you have already massively increased your chances of success, there is still more you can be doing, there are still additional strategies you can bring to your game; there are still my 'super secret advanced techniques'!

So let's take a look at these additional techniques one by one and remember, they build on what you have already put into place. They build on the earlier chapters of this book and, using a boxing analogy, are the knockout blows at the end of the fight!

LinkedIn Labs - Signal

LinkedIn Labs is an area of LinkedIn that in my experience few people seem to know about, let alone use!

LinkedIn Labs (**www.linkedinlabs.com**) hosts a collection of projects and experimental applications built by the employees of LinkedIn. These applications, while not part of the main LinkedIn platform, can be used in conjunction with your existing LinkedIn profile. One of the most powerful tools lurking in LinkedIn Labs is Signal (**www.linkedinlabs.com/signal**).

Signal is a tool that you can use to filter, interrogate and make sense of the never ending stream of LinkedIn 'Status Updates'. Imagine if you could find the status updates in your geographical area that talk about hiring, recruiting and employment. If you could easily pinpoint these posts, you could respond and get directly to the people on LinkedIn who are recruiting now, the people who want to find people like you with skills and experience to offer.

The good news is that you can do all of this and more with LinkedIn Signal. Once accessed from LinkedIn Labs, Signal becomes part of your profile with a navigation bar down the left hand side of your status updates that allow you to filter as follows:

- Search box – try the words 'hiring' or 'recruiting'.

- Network – select which connections you want to include in your status update search. My advice is to keep this as wide as possible and include everyone.

- Company – you can drill right down into status updates from employees of a particular company, or leave this unchecked to search all companies.

- Location – this is where the search gets really powerful as you can add particular geographical areas, select them and pull up results for the locations you are interested in.

On Signal you're likely to pull up filtered results and status updates posted by businesses hiring directly and also professional recruiters representing organisations. What's fantastic is that through the 'Comment' box you can communicate directly, in real time, with the hiring manager or recruiter – now how powerful is that?!

Leverage

Remember Greg in Chapter 7? Greg approached my business offering to help with our PR and marketing. We weren't hiring or looking for external help in this area but have now employed Greg's services for over two years. Greg's approach is a great example of using leverage.

Leverage has numerous definitions, but for our purposes it's the power or ability to influence others and, most importantly, to influence the decisions they make.

Another example springs to mind that may help illustrate this point further.

We are currently running a process to bring new recruitment consultants into our business. Yes, I know, good news as when recruiters are hiring staff for their businesses, the market must really be picking up! Anyway, a candidate approached me; let's call him Charles. He sent his CV to me and then followed up his application up with a phone call. Charles was quite persuasive, but given his level of experience (he's run his own recruitment business in the past) I was not convinced there was a good match for our organisation and I declined a meeting.

What Charles did next was very clever and a great example of leverage. Charles forwarded me an email he had sent to one of his former clients introducing my business and our services – he's opened the door through his network to a client we had never worked with before.

A few days later, Charles sent me another email with the contact details of someone else he knew in the market that was actively recruiting for a temporary member of staff. Again, he had gone out of his way to help my business and to help us build new and potentially fruitful relationships. Charles had also demonstrated to me the power of his network. There's a well known phrase, which says, *"It's not what you know, it's who you know!"*

So what do you think happened next? Well, I invited Charles in for a meeting. Charles through the clever use of leverage had achieved his goal of getting in front of me, the decision maker.

So what can you learn from Greg and now Charles? There will be leverage you can use in your industry to help you get in front of the decision maker. It may not be obvious immediately, but spend some time, think about it and there will be ways and means for you to influence the decision makers you want and need to get in front of – trust me on this one!

Blog/Industry expert

Whether you are familiar with the term 'blog' or not you've probably read one without even knowing it. A blog is a website which contains a writer's observations, experiences and thoughts on a given subject. I write a blog for our website which contains my thoughts on what's happening in the employment market. It also highlights things we are doing as a recruitment business, such as events, courses and awards. For anyone looking to find work or to understand more about our business, it's a potentially interesting read. It's also a great way to keep in regular contact with our target audience of clients and candidates.

"So what does this have to do with me?" I hear you ask.

Well, it has everything to do with you. Whatever industry or sector you work in, whatever your job title or skill set, you have knowledge, expertise and something to say. You don't need to be the best writer or linguist, trust me I'm not, but you need an opinion and thoughts that you can communicate to others.

But before I talk about how to set up a blog, why bother?

Let's run through a quick example (as you'll have noticed by now, I'm quite fond of examples to bring things to life):

Julie is a Mechanical Engineer; she's out of work and looking for that next opportunity. She has worked in the industry for many years and has lots of knowledge. Julie also keeps up to speed with the latest developments in the Mechanical Engineering world and reads the latest publications and news. As a result, she has information to share with the outside world and decides to write a blog. Each day she writes a few paragraphs on a topic of her choice and posts it on the internet. She does this consistently and as such, builds up a bank of valuable content on Mechanical Engineering.

Julie is bright, spots opportunity and uses her blog to promote her skills and to help her find her next job in the following ways:

- She links her blog to LinkedIn – LinkedIn allows you to highlight a website on your profile and visitors to Julie's profile can now see how knowledgeable she is on Mechanical Engineering.

- In communications online with prospective employers she can include a link to her blog. It's something different and unique that other jobseekers won't be doing and provides an excellent platform for her to sell her skills.

Blogs sit on the internet and anything sitting on the internet is searchable. In her blog Julie will be using words specific to the Mechanical Engineering sector. At regular intervals Google will visit her website to understand what she is talking about, so it can provide the most relevant search results to its customers. As Julie is writing a blog, her content changes on a regular basis (often daily) which means that Google visits her blog on a frequent basis in order to understand what has changed. Julie can now be found not only on LinkedIn but also on her own website – she can be found by people interested in Mechanical Engineering who might just be hiring or people who know someone that is!

Through her blog Julie has positioned herself as an industry expert and is producing interesting and relevant content that has a personality – her personality. You can do the same!

There are many websites out there that allow you to create a blog very quickly, and for free, including:

Blogger – **www.blogger.com**

WordPress – **www.wordpress.com**

I particularly like WordPress, as through the LinkedIn WordPress Application, you can sync your WordPress blog posts with your LinkedIn profile. (There is also another LinkedIn Application called Blog Link that allows you to link other blogs.) Your blog automatically feeds your LinkedIn profile with regular and highly relevant content – how good is that?!

Race to Face

In Chapter 7 I discussed how to get in front of the decision maker. The name of the game is always to get a face to face meeting. Remember, people hire people and not bits of paper (CVs), so getting up close and personal is essential.

Throughout this book I have guided you through the recruitment process and you've built your road map to find your next job. What if I told you that it's possible to take a detour that cuts out some of the journey and can get you to your destination much quicker – would you believe me and would you take it? You see there is a shortcut, but the road can be bumpy and sometimes jobseekers are afraid to take it. This is great news! It's difficult so your competition, namely other jobseekers, avoid it. But it's possible and if you brave the bumpy road you have an even greater chance of success!

I call this 'Race to Face' and I'll now show you how.

Having set out your road map and identified the businesses where you can add value and that you want to work for, instead of email, letter and other forms of communication take the bull by the horns and go visit. Yes, that's right, go visit!

Put on your best suit, print a copy of your super CV and turn up. Do you care if there is a job or not? No, you don't because you are confident in your skills and in your ability to add value to the business you are visiting. You have done all the preparation discussed in earlier chapters, you have prepared for the interview, you know whom to ask for and you're ready for action!

You might think I'm crazy, but I know from experience that I'm not. A number of years ago, a guy turned up at my office. He hadn't made an appointment and he hadn't called in advance. He simply turned up and asked for me by name at reception.

I was intrigued and came out to meet him. Jon was well dressed and greeted me with a beaming smile and firm handshake. He explained that he'd recently moved back to the area and had heard good things about my business and our abilities to help people find work – I was instantly flattered.

I bought Jon a coffee and we sat down and chatted for 20 minutes. He walked me through his CV, highlighting his key achievements and was clear in explaining the types of positions he was looking for – I was impressed.

Jon had unusual experience; he had qualified as an accountant but had then completely left the profession to take on a pizza business franchise. For the last two years he had been running a pizza takeaway and doing everything from making pizza to mopping floors!

On paper Jon didn't look like a candidate I could help. He had been out of the accountancy game for a couple of years; he'd trained with an average firm and didn't have a fantastic academic record by his own admission. To be honest, I never would have met him and the only reason I did was because he turned up in reception unannounced. However, his drive, enthusiasm and personality (all hard to convey in written word) shone through and it became my mission to help him find his next move.

To cut a long story short I placed Jon in a job with a great business and his career has gone from strength to strength ever since. He called me not so long ago to let me know he'd been promoted, had received a salary increase and was taking delivery of a brand new Mercedes! Jon is a prime example of someone who took control of his own destiny and has reaped the rewards because of his courage and determination.

'Race to Face' is a great way to get ahead of the competition and to find your next job quickly, but it requires courage. Sure, it's not always plain sailing. The person you are after might not be in or may be unwilling to come and meet you – expect this, as it will happen.

But guess what? You still have an opportunity to impress the receptionist and to drop off your CV. The receptionist and the decision maker talk and if you are professional, polite and courteous this message will get through.

I challenge you to include this technique in your job search strategy. Don't worry if you fail at the first attempt. Say to yourself you will try this technique ten times at least and I'm certain you will find success and grow in confidence as a result.

As someone once told me, "*fortune favours the brave!*"

Final
THOUGHTS

The purpose of my book has been to help you the jobseeker stand out from the crowd and to take planned and structured action in your life to achieve success in finding your next job. Why you are looking for a new position, whether it be due to redundancy or the desire for career development is of less concern. What is important is how you think, feel and act and most importantly WHAT YOU CHOOSE TO DO NOW!

Having finished my book, you are now at your most empowered, but are also at that danger point of doing nothing! Ever been on a course and come away with a whole host of new ideas and things you are going to do, but never get round to doing any of them? I think if we're honest with ourselves we all have!

Tomorrow is the first day of the rest of your career, so start now and take the steps I've outlined to take control of your life and your job search. It's your responsibility; you are the commander of your ship and where you choose to steer it is up to you. Be accountable and be empowered! Make sure you enjoy the journey and not just the destination, and most of all have fun!

In my introduction I said that life is all about effective relationships and it is. Your success is about getting face to face and communicating your value clearly and concisely. Motivation doesn't keep you doing something, but habit does, so set your road map and focus on the journey.

Don't be deterred and know that hard work and commitment pays off!

THE START!

For the latest information, ongoing support and for further discussion on the topics covered in this book please visit: **www.supersecretsofthesuccessfuljobseeker.com**.

APPENDIX
CV TEMPLATE

NAME:	Simon Cherry
RESIDENCE:	Town or City – Willing to relocate?
EDUCATION:	Degree (e.g. BSc, BA (Hons), MSc etc) – subject – class (e.g. 2.1, 2.2)
	A Levels or equivalent – subject and grades (e.g. Maths A, English A, Physics B)
	GCSEs/O Levels or equivalent – number (subject and grades not needed)
PROFESSIONAL QUALIFICATIONS:	Include pass record/awards if relevant
LANGUAGES:	List languages – spoken/written – fluent/intermediate/basic

EXPERIENCE:

NOV 2003 – DATE	**COMPANY OR ORGANISATION**
	Brief description of the company, what it does, sector, turnover of group and division.
MAR 2006 – DATE	**Job Title**
	Responsibilities:
	(List 3 or 4 key responsibilities)
	Who did you report to?
	What did you do on a daily basis?
	Staff management (size of your team and what level, number of direct and indirect reports)?

Achievements (READY?):

(List 3 or 4 key achievements)

Value add example 1

Value add example 2

Value add example 3

NOV 2003 –
FEB 2006

Job Title

Responsibilities:

(List 3 or 4 key responsibilities)

Who did you report to?

What did you do on a daily basis?

Staff management (size of your team and what level, number of direct and indirect reports)?

Achievements (READY?):

(List 3 or 4 key achievements)

Value add example 1

Value add example 2

Value add example 3

COMPUTER/IT
SKILLS:

Systems used and to what level?

Microsoft Office?

INTERESTS:

What do you do in your spare time and to what level?

Index

B

Blogger 147
blogging 146-147
business plan, your 4, 35-36
  being accountable for 41
  budgeting 39
  components of 43-46
  daily action plans, *see* 'daily action plans'
  destination of 37
  empowering others 40, 41
  exercise, importance of 43-44
  foundations of 37-43
  going out 44
  knowing when to stop 44-45
  prospective employers 38
  reason for search 37-38
  rest, need for 41-43
  timescales 39-40
  type of job sought 38
  visualisation 43
  writing it down 40-41

C

communication
  email, via 106-107
  following up 112-115
  letter, via 109-111
  phone, via 111
  social media, via 107-109

competition 13
covering letters 31
CVs
  achievements 26-27
    example 27
  adding value to 22-23, 26
  computer/IT skills 24, 28
    example 28
  design of 31
  education 23, 24
  experts 18
  FAQs 31-32
  hobbies/interests 24, 28-29
  importance of ix
  job titles, importance of 25-26
  judgements of 21
  languages 23
  length of 32
  personal information 23, 24
  personal summaries 31
  photos, and 32
  purpose of 18, 19
  READY?, *see* 'READY?'
  relocation 24
  qualifications 23, 24-25
  readers of 20-23
  responsibilities 26
  spelling and grammar 30
  starting again 17
  target audience of 20
  technical jargon, and 21